The Temple is YOU

BRINGING IN THE LIGHT SERIES

Book III

The Temple is YOU

Copyright © 2024 by the Author,
John Pollock

The Temple is YOU is self-published by the author.

The Temple is YOU

FIRST EDITION

BRINGING IN THE LIGHT SERIES
Book III

Copyright © 2024 John Pollock

The book author retains sole copyright to his
contributions to this book and series

The Temple is YOU is written and self-published by the author, John Pollock.
All Prayers, Affirmations, and Invocations are channeled by the author unless
otherwise noted.

Edited by Jennifer Sweete with author

Cover Art & Design by Jennifer Sweete, Copyright © John Pollock

Illustrated by John Pollock
Channeled Light Photo Design by Carol Skylark
Clipart from Public Domain
All Other Acknowledgments within Chapters

Soft Cover:
13 ISBN: 978-0-9984448-4-0

"Our personal connection with God is for our personal growth along our path.
The other experiences in life are to enrich and support our growth."

- John Pollock

The Love in our hearts is a silent prayer.

Continue this amazing journey
with me in this
Bringing In the Light Series!

Visit my website at
www.AngelsGrace.org
to obtain more books in this series.

Prayers for All Occasions
BRINGING IN THE LIGHT SERIES
Book I

MYSTIC: Manifesting Your Soul,
Truth In Consciousness
BRINGING IN THE LIGHT SERIES
Book II

The Temple Is YOU
BRINGING IN THE LIGHT SERIES
Book III

Dedication

This book is dedicated to Athene Raefiel

who continually inspires me

toward greater understanding

of higher realms.

Table of Contents

"Spirit working through us to raise the vibration
of humanity's spiritual essence to a higher consciousness
is the pathway to evolution."

- John Pollock

Preface

I have been on a spiritual quest and a great adventure since before the harmonic convergence in 1987. I experienced a great Christ healing and personal awakening in the Light. At first, I spent many hours adjusting to the intense energies which seemed to stay with me and bring surprise experiences and synchronicities into my life. Since that awakening, I have been constantly questioning what was happening to me and anxiously awaiting what would happen next.

In my earlier life, I would have thoughts and make plans, then proceed forward. I had two daughters and went through a divorce, so I was concerned with raising a family, building a career, and exploring relationships. My first priority was raising my two kids.

After the awakening, I was living on a different level. It was some kind of half-meditative state. I was still able to function in ordinary life, but I would be frequently energized in a higher realm. I was guided toward people with whom I shared spiritual purpose. This experience of awakening helped me to open up to share Higher Love and Christ Light.

In every situation in life, I would figure out what the higher purpose might have been and try to see things from a higher spiritual perspective.

Since my awakening with Christ Light, I have been carrying more Light in my personal energy field. I found that I could balance other people's energy fields, and I started having visions of Christ and Mother Mary.

As my experiences expanded, I began offering spiritual healing to others, bridging the gap between this physical expression and a client's own etheric guidance with Christ Holy Spirit. After several years of facilitating in Colorado, Arizona, and Florida, I returned home to the Denver area where I spent a number of years caring for my aging mother.

Along my journey, I was accumulating inspirational articles that I had been writing throughout the years while facilitating clients. It seemed like a natural next step to gather many of them together into my book *Prayers for All Occasions,* a book that was born to present prayers and invocations to assist everyone to infuse more Light into their lives, and my first book in this series called "Bringing In the Light." I was sharing what I learned from my connection with Spirit, assisting others to connect in meditation and teaching, and helping others to heal.

The second book in the series is called *MYSTIC: Manifesting Your Soul, Truth in Consciousness.* It teaches how to work with Spirit and carry more Light in our energy field. Our prayer and meditation raise our vibration rate. In meditation, we reach up to the Mind of God, bring the Light down to what Hermes calls the ONE THING, and surrender our life to our higher purpose. We ask for miracles and expect the best! Light fills our soul energy field and energizes our life on the physical plane. This attracts synchronicity and grace to our flow, as well as empowering our life with Spirit.

The first book teaches praying to Christ Holy Spirit and Angels, and aligning with Higher Light. The second book teaches how we align with our soul level and guidance to bring a lighter, more loving expression into our experiences—personal mastery through alignment with Higher Light.

As the third book in the "Bringing in the Light" series, *The Temple is YOU* takes spiritual evolution to the next level. Each of us is responsible for releasing our own emotional baggage. We always place ourselves into the Light to know and understand our spiritual path. We learn by blending our spiritual essence with Higher Light and ask for assistance to be lifted to Higher levels of Light. This happens through the Grace of God when we are open to receive greater Love.

There is legend of a race called the Hathors who ascended together into the Light. I once met with three or four fellow Light workers after a large group meeting and was led to bring up the subject of the Hathors. What a surprise as we all felt the strong and loving energies bless our group! I wondered, *How will humanity ever evolve to release their stifling attachments to the material world, and attain such ascension into the Light?*

By exploring the origins of many religions, we gain perspective and a deeper understanding of our personal connection with Spirit.

Proverbs 16:9 says, "A man's heart deviseth his way: but the LORD directeth his steps." We each must use discernment when regarding Free Will. We can be certain which voice is God's voice when we are present in higher consciousness, transcending the pitfalls and issues of *mass* consciousness. Discernment is a gift from the Holy Spirit into our hearts, telling us whether something is right for us, as opposed to our personalities' judgments of situations or people. Being reborn in Spirit is not earned, but rather a gift given to us when we are ready to receive this highest of blessings.

Upon awakening to the Light, our energy field and soul are charged and infused with Christ Holy Spirit. We are then drawn to the Beings of Light that we can relate to. We embark on our very own path of self-discovery and enlightenment.

The purpose of this book is to remind us that within each of us our own Temple that is the Self within the Light, illuminates our path of spiritual evolution and, through Spirit, brings tools for us to explore possibilities for the ascension of all humanity.

Please join me on this amazing spiritual journey to discovering *The Temple is YOU!*

"Being reborn in Spirit is not earned,
but rather a gift given to us when we are ready
to receive this highest of blessings."

- John Pollock

Acknowledgments

The books in the "Bringing in the Light" series—*Prayers for All Occasions,* and *MYSTIC: Manifest Your Soul, Truth in Consciousness,* and this latest book *The Temple is YOU!* have all unfolded before me in perfect order. I was divinely inspired to title these books as a set called the "Bringing in the Light" series long before I had finished the first book *Prayers for All Occasions.* I was not totally sure how many books would follow. This journey has been continual surprises from Spirit!

I am grateful for thirty years of participating in the healing for humankind, but most of all, for being in service to the Light and expanding consciousness in myself. The information in *Prayers for All Occasions* came as inspiration during the facilitation of healing sessions over thirty years as a spiritual and angelic healer.

When I received the idea to put the information from healing work together in a book, I didn't have a clue of what was to come next. Since that time, I have been following guidance to present one book at a time. Each book has its own level of consciousness, and you can tell that my guidance consists of different beings of Light working together in concert. All the information fits together to further our spiritual growth.

In the process of merging with Christ Holy Spirit and Angel consciousness, I have learned that, like the Angels, we all have a common purpose to express higher vibrations of Love in service to Spirit in the Light.

The Archangels Raphael, Michael, Gabriel, and Uriel work directly with humankind. Along with other Angel consciousness, they come to me in inspiration, calling to Christ Holy Spirit and Archangels to anchor the four cardinal directions of the medicine wheel teachings and higher wisdom, lifting humankind higher in consciousness. This teaching is the basis for teaching personal alignment with our truth within, through our soul and higher self, Divine Father and Mother God, to the purest heart of Love and Light of all creation and "All That Is." Getting grounded is connecting with Mother Earth for nurturing and support, balancing with Spirit into the physical, and aligning with Light for empowerment.

I give thanks for the personal relationships I've developed with the Angels in my healing work and my teachings in *Prayers for All Occasions*.

Teachings are carried forward in *MYSTIC: Manifesting Your Soul, Truth in Consciousness*. Wisdom for manifesting our spiritual path using prayer, invocation, and other spiritual tools given to us, help us to raise our spiritual essence in our physical expression.

In this third book *The Temple is YOU,* the teachings of the Ascended Masters shine through in our personal quest for transformation. The ascended masters include Djwhal Khul the Tibetan, El Moya, Kathumi, Serapis Bay, Paul the Venetian, Hilarion, Sananda, St. Germain and Lady Master Nada. Of course, all teachings in the Light work together to bring wisdom at all levels to move us forward in our personal quest.

I give my profound thanks to Spirit for expanding consciousness, blessing my path of service, and bringing me together with people whom I am able to bring Light through for healing and teaching, helping everyone possible. Light comes through synchronicities in my life-expression, bringing miracles to us all. My flow of Light through the right people in the physical world facilitates moving ahead on my spiritual path, many times at blazing speed.

Jennifer Sweete deserves honorable mention for her editing of all my books, as well as, for working with higher energies that are operating within the writing of wisdom and consciousness always given to us in appropriate timing for blessing humankind by the Angels and all bringers of Light.

Athene Raefiel has brought insight and higher understanding of different realms to the workings of Light and Love in the universe. Her support has always been much appreciated. I've always seen her as an Angel working for the Light here on Earth.

I thank my good friend and neighbor Rosa for sharing prayer and friendship about life and aspects of relationships.

I want to thank my good friend, Ann Swenson, who recently crossed over. Together, we worked with issues around aging and life extension firsthand. She and her loving contribution of insights on healing and prayer will be greatly missed in this physical world, though her strong presence is still with us.

I am forever grateful to my two daughters, angels-incarnate in my life since they were born! Their love and support throughout my many adventures in life, including my writing adventures, have been my highest inspirations on Earth!

I would also like to thank my sister who has been a constant in my life, a wonderful sounding board, guide, and support.

Thank you to all of you who read these books and share them and the truths brought forth in them for living in the Light of Love.

Blessings,
John

"Our potential for growth is unlimited."

- John Pollock

CHAPTER I — I AM, WE ARE

In the course of being born and living a life on the Earth plane, members of the human race experience taking on judgments, values, beliefs, and even different religions from society. Issues are shared by the masses and experienced by individuals the world over to be replayed in their lives until such time as they are released from mass consciousness one individual at a time.

In a world of duality, our focus is constantly diverted by the outside world to encourage participation and struggles with our love-lives, acceptance, money, power, fame, possessions, and control over others.

The purpose of the many religions throughout history has been the lifting of our consciousness and the raising of our awareness from the three-dimensional world outside ourselves, to knowing our Divine self and true happiness in union with Spirit. Whether in individual or group meditation, we access Spirit through our *feeling-body* and flow to our place of inner peace. We bring attention to our breath, the subtle vibration of energy, and the colors with higher meaning that we see in our third eye, much like colors we experience in dream-state.

We come to realize, with years of life experience, that everyone is here on Earth for their own spiritual journey and their own agenda. At soul-level, we are attracting our own experiences and learning the things we've come here to learn. Each life is about expansion of consciousness, sharing love in its many forms of varied expression, and connecting with higher dimensions on our journey to return home to Source God.

We may choose the adventures in life that seem exciting at first; however, life in the fast lane can bring some harsh lessons along with the excitement. As we grow, we may eventually feel overwhelmed with the experiences we are attracting. Sooner or later, we want to bring ourselves a more graceful, fulfilling, and gentler lifestyle. When we get to the point of seeking more grace and looking for more love to come into our lives, we start asking Spirit to bring us blessings from higher dimensions and higher wisdom to guide us past the pitfalls of the "exciting" dramatic lives we were previously choosing.

Without realizing, the intent to be closer to Spirit works as a magnet to bring more Light and more grace into our lives. Our desire to know God better serves as a prayer to Spirit to bring in more Light, Love, and higher guidance. Spirit is responsive to the desires and the yearning in our hearts. Beings of Light and Angels bless our lives as we begin to share Light with others. Miracles spontaneously appear in our lives, blessing our path and bringing grace.

At first, the prayers that we say every day raise our vibration rate. Still, we are pleasantly surprised when we realize just how positively they affect us. Light brings synchronicities and gentle gifts from Spirit into our flow.

When we decide to pursue a path toward enlightenment, there are things we can do to enhance our journey. The first is to surrender our personality-driven will and ask that our personal energies be blended with the gentle flow of the Holy Spirit and spiritual guidance.

The second is to call to the Light to set up a medicine wheel vortex to infuse more Light into our lives. We call Christ Holy Spirit, the Archangels, and Beings of Light with whom we have a deep connection. We are saying prayers for assistance to create a Sacred Space for Holy communion, turning over situations and concerns to God for charging our energy field with Light, for healing for ourselves and others, and for guidance in our lives.

It is beneficial to know that we can align with Light and higher dimensions, and that our prayers can work to program our lives, if only we ask. We align with our truth within our heart, and align with Spirit on all levels. The energetic healing procedures and the work with our spiritual flow are much the same. Our potential for growth is unlimited, and our success is *only* limited by our creative imagination with Spirit.

Our love within is empowered by our energy field to attract blessings for us to experience grace. Our issues will attract harsh lessons if our beliefs are projecting that reality. It is up to us to program a reality of grace with Spirit and fulfillment with our prayers. Helping others whenever we can, and keeping a good sense of humor, helps us experience the best.

We experience the energies of our soul as a solid connection that remains constant in support of our life-expression and allows for the influx of Light from higher dimensions, bringing in our higher soul's purpose with guidance to manifest our highest expression.

To understand how this process works through us and for us, we can look at the ancient religious teachings as they continue to evolve into modern religious practices, and take from them the knowledge of personal transformation and ascension—direct contact with Source God, the **ONE MIND**—becoming our own Philosopher's Stone, a temple of Higher Truth.

IN EXPRESSING OUR SOUL PURPOSE,

WE ARE UPLIFTING OURSELVES

AND ALL OF HUMANITY.

I AM, WE ARE.

"The three aspects of worship are,
as they have always been:
Power, Wisdom, and Love."

- John Pollock

Ancient Temples and Early Cultures

The history of planet Earth has seen the rise and fall of many civilizations. Ancient history and spiritual doctrine appear to start with the legend of the Sun Temple in Atlantis. The Sun Temple combined three aspects of worship in one tradition. This was prior to the sinking of the lost continent of Atlantis below the Atlantic Ocean. Before the great cataclysm there were three religious and cultural migrations that each transferred part of the teaching to other places in the world. Each had their own characteristics that predominated.

The three aspects of worship are, as they have always been: Power, Wisdom, and Love.

The first exodus migration from Atlantis, that of Power, was the basis for primitive magic where initiations only reach the lower astral plane. The energies move up from below. Primitive tribes in Central America are known to have carried out human sacrifice and have misqualified the energies to control members of the tribe, using abuse of prisoners and psychedelic potions to create magic with nature. Witch doctors are included in this group. Many still use primitive ritual ceremonies and prayer with voodoo dolls.

The second exodus migration from Atlantis was that of Wisdom, traveling to central Asia and the Himalayas. Some of the most profound knowledge in the world has been guarded and kept secret in the mountain retreats. Teachings from these places, such as Tibet and India, involve meditation, discipline, and dedication.

The third great exodus from Atlantis took place just before the sinking of the land mass itself. It was the tradition called Love, traveling to the Mediterranean Basin and the Near East. The Greek mysteries and the mysteries of freemasonry from the Phoenician city of Tyra were received from the Egyptians. From the early influence of Tyra, we received the Hebrew tradition. From the Greek Mysteries came the Gnosis that was to become known in the future as Alchemy. The teachings of Jesus are in the tradition of Love.

It takes all three traditions to combine into the original whole Sun Ray to raise our spirituality in enlightenment. Power brings compassion, beauty, and a connection with nature from the Celts. The Wisdom from God comes through a strong meditative tradition of discipline and dedication. Love comes from the Hebrew initiations on the TREE OF LIFE. Gnosis expands the heart flame within. Christ forgiveness and Buddha compassion of Chenrizig reside in this heart flame. It all has Buddha consciousness and Christ Holy Spirit at the core.

Earth has an energy system that comes from God infusing Light. Many people are unaware that there is a flow of electromagnetic energy in and around Earth that supports life on our planet. The energy lines, called ley lines, crisscross the planet in a grid system, creating energy vortexes—very much like the energy system of the human body, which also has energy vortexes that we call chakras. Just as Earth's vortexes, our chakras are interconnected and have different purposes.

Where the ley lines of Earth's energy cross each other, we have high energy spots and vortex locations. In the past, these high energy locations were ideal to establish temples and meeting structures for ritual prayer gatherings. Even now, priests choose locations that have high energy for meeting places, where the strong energies from Mother Earth assist humankind in connecting with Spirit at higher and higher levels in meditation. These high energy spots are often investigated in conjunction with ancient temple sites of old.

Gobekli Tepe

Gobekli Tepe is the oldest known archaeological site in the world to date. It is located in the southeastern area of Turkey, seven miles northeast of the city of Sanhurfa. It was discovered in an artificial mound fifty feet high and one thousand feet across, and was radiocarbon dated back to 12,000 years ago—6,000 years before the construction of Stonehenge. This is older than the use of pottery and before agriculture was conceived. It has been concluded that the main purpose for the structure was for use as a regional meeting place.

Gobekli Tepe is constructed in a circle with twelve massive Limestone pillars in a "T" shape, the largest up to twenty-three feet tall and ten feet wide, with some weighing as much as fifty tons. The walls were made of stones, each about the size of a brick. These were glued together with clay and used to fill in between the pillars, forming the walls of the ceremonial circle. There were two large stones in the center of the temple.

Carbon dating indicates the original enclosures were backfilled during the Stone Age, though it is unknown why. New construction was built inside the old structures.

Up to the writing of this book, there have been twenty circles uncovered in Gobekli Tepe. Many have been built in later additions. Whereas the oldest construction was built in a circle, subsequent phases were built in rectangular design and geometrically situated in a triangular formation.

A fourth phase was built above the first three, with hundreds of years passing in between additions. Living quarters were built in back, to the north, west, and east.

Sacred Geometry was used in the layout of the structure, giving us insight toward the prayers and rituals that took place there. It is clear this was a spiritual center where sacred geometry, accompanied by prayer, was used to raise the vibration of the place and the people.

Archeologists have determined from building construction that sacrifice was not part of rituals performed there. The main function of the kiva construction was for gathering and ritual ceremonies oriented to the stars and constellations. The full nature and knowledge of Power, Wisdom, and Love in their culture is not yet known.

Lalibela

L alibela is a small town in Ethiopia with long, winding mountain roads. The people there feel that the Lalibela pilgrimage shares the same blessing as the pilgrimage to Jerusalem.

There are twelve spectacular churches in and around the town of Lalibela. Each was carved out of solid rock over nine hundred years ago. The Ethiopian Orthodox Church attracts eighty to a hundred thousand visitors every year. Every church in Lalibela, even after all these centuries, is fully functioning and still offers services every day.

The churches are four-story structures with high ceilings. Each was carved inside and out from the mountain rock, starting at the top and cutting away a space around the structure, leaving the church still standing inside the solid rock of the mountain. The shape of the structure that is left is in the shape of a cross, four stories tall. It is a living historical testament to God.

Religious worship there is an extension of Christianity, and an extension of Wisdom and Love rays of old. This spiritual center has always used prayer and ritual to raise the vibration of the place and the people.

Anasazi

Ancient Anasazi ruins are located in the four corners area of the United States, known as Chaco Canyon, where Arizona, New Mexico, Colorado, and Utah join together. The Anasazi civilization extended to Mesa Verde, Canyon Du Chelly, Tower Utah, and east on the high Colorado Plateau. The Navajo Indians gave them their name "Anasazi," which means Ancient Ones.

The Anasazi area operated as a hub for Native American tribes trading goods throughout the southwest.

Archaeologists have dated a booming civilization there from 100 AD to 1300 AD, coming to an end with a drought in 1276 AD that lasted until 1299 AD. The area was uninhabited for seven hundred years after that.

The Pueblo Indians told us that the Anasazi worshipped the sun and nature and the sacredness of Mother Earth. The Native American tribes of today say that they respect the spirits that can still be felt in the Anasazi dwellings and ceremonial kivas.

To feel the energy of the spirits, visitors are told to connect in their mind, heart, and body. The spirits are still blessing people with their higher dimensional prayers that offer blessings for their children and blessings for a long life.

Petroglyphs carry messages through images—the most familiar being Kokopelli, the fertility god. Broken pottery cluttered the floors in the ceremonial kivas as an offering to the spirits in prayer. Neighboring tribes knew not to pick up the pottery because the pottery was broken as sacred offering to the spirits who still remain there and still carry prayers for others.

There is an opening in the center of the kiva known as the Cava Pool. This opening descends down and then comes back up and above the kiva. The shaman leading the ceremony would take this path down and would magically appear in the center of the kiva during ceremony.

The culture centered around trade with other tribes that were coming and going. The worship was an extension of the Wisdom and Love rays of old, focusing on the stars, constellations, the Sun, and nature.

This was a Native American spiritual center where ceremony and prayer were used to raise the vibration of the place and the people, blessing all who lived there and traveled there for trade.

Greece

Greece is located north of the Mediterranean Sea with Italy to the west, Turkey to the east, and Egypt to the south.

Today, the ancient religion in Greece that once worshipped the pantheon of twelve gods on Mount Olympus over three thousand years ago, has blended with the Angels and Saints of Christianity that formally formed approximately two thousand years ago with the coming of Jesus Christ.

The apostle John went into seclusion in caves in the island of Patmos off the coast of Greece. It was there that John received Divine inspiration to see the apocalypse that was coming, and to write the last chapter of the Bible New Testament called the "Book of Revelation." He saw the second coming of Christ and judgment day.

The ancient buildings are still standing and honor the twelve gods of the pantheon with winged angels. The ruins of the Acropolis still have faces and statues of the gods. Walkways in Delphi still lead to ruins and buildings for meetings with the Oracle of Delphi, Apollo and Athena, who were highly sought after for prophecy.

Mount Olympus still remains, and the Parthenon still stands on the Acropolis of Athens with spiritual geometric design for worship. This was one of the earliest uses of spiritual geometry. The Parthenon was built to honor Athena, daughter of Zeus, Goddess of Wisdom and War, and protector of Athens. North of the Parthenon was built the rection with six angels who were servants giving tribute to Goddess Athena. The angels were similar to the angels found on the Isle of Capri.

Some of the most powerful of the Greek gods were written about in great detail:

Zeus, with his lightning bolt of the flame of divine awareness, was known as the most respected and powerful of all the ancient Greek gods.

Poseidon was the god of the sea, possessing the trident bearing the three points of power—Faith, Love, and Hope.

16

Much misunderstood *Hades,* the god of the underworld, provided temporary accommodations for souls traveling between worlds. The underworld is often mistaken for that which we call Hell, though they are not the same.

Apollo with his rays of enlightenment was known as the god of poetry, art, and prophecy, and the Greeks compared him to Christ.

Hermes, emissary and messenger of the gods, held the caduceus representing connection and healing. The Greek Pistis Sophia was a major third century Gnostic text with the Hermetic teachings that deal with all the levels Jesus had to travel through in His ascension.

The Greek teachings were an extension of ancient teachings emigrating to Europe, including the Wisdom and Love rays.

Israel, Jerusalem

Israel is bound by Syria to the north, Jordan to the east, and Egypt to the west. Jerusalem is the capital of Israel with three different religions that claim the city as sacred. Judaism, Christianity, and the Muslim religion. The city is occupied by half a million people congested in a space of about one square mile, yet somehow in all the confusion, they make it work.

Four thousand years ago in Israel, the God Yahweh spoke to Abraham and tested his faith. Then, in 70 AD, the temple to Yahweh fulfilled prophecy of being destroyed by the Romans. The only thing left standing was the West Wall, which the Jewish people viewed as triumph over death. The West Wall is sacred, preserving the temple to Yahweh. The Jewish people have always referred to the sanctuary as Temple Mount. The most sacred site of all is the inner sanctuary *within* the sanctuary that is referred to as the "Holy of Holies." The Jewish people see the city of Jerusalem as the Promised Land.

Muslims have a story where the Archangel Gabriel came to Muhammed and took him on a mystical journey to the same location as Temple Mount, which the Muslims call Makkah Noble, meaning "The Sanctuary." It was there that Muhammed tied up his horse and climbed up a stairway of Light to Heaven where he united with his God, Allah.

The Muslims face to the east and pray five times per day. They believe that their own temple on Temple Mount, which they call "Mecca," is the most holy temple on Earth.

Similar to the ancient Egyptians, the Koran says that, in the end times, humanity is judged by the heaviness of their hearts upon a scale. Their hearts are weighed against the lightness of a white feather.

Christians there have the Monastery of the Cross. They also have the road leading to the place of crucifixion with stations along the way. It is called Via Delarosa, "the way of sorrow." At the end of the road is the Church of the Holy Sepulchre to honor the death, burial, and resurrection of Jesus Christ. It was there that the body of Jesus was washed and prepared for burial.

For Christians, the death and resurrection of Jesus brings the message that there is everlasting life after death. After His resurrection, the stone was gone from in front of His tomb and He appeared in His energetic body to the apostles, demonstrating that the spiritual essence of humankind is eternal. He showed that there is triumph over death in the physical, and that those who believe in Him shall never die. Jesus tells us of His second coming and that there will be a judgment day.

The apostles were told by Jesus to think of Him and partake of bread representing His flesh, and partake of wine representing His blood. This ritual ceremony was and is still called "communion." The life of Jesus Christ is the demonstration of the Power of Love and Wisdom.

Egypt

The history of Egypt is said by some to be five thousand years old, though others believe the pyramids to be much older. The Sphinx is chiseled out of one rock, and though it is dated even older than the so-called "5000-year-old" pyramids, actually archaeologists still cannot determine with any certainty how old it may really be.

Egypt is bordered by the Mediterranean Sea to the north, Libya to the west, Sudan to the south, and Saudi Arabia to the east. Egyptians have worshipped the flow of the Nile River as Egypt's only source of water, bringing fertile soil every time Egypt is flooded.

The pharaohs were worshipped as the interpreters between the afterlife in the Above and the living people of the country in the Below. It is believed that the people were participating with the pharaohs to build the pyramids and would receive a good life for their participation.

Around the fourth century BCE, around the time of Alexander the Great, Egypt was reborn in the Islamic faith. It was felt that in death their hearts would be weighed against a white feather by the god Anubis, recorded by Thoth, and reported to Osiris. If it came out favorably, it would ensure that the people would experience a more pleasant afterlife with peace and prosperity.

In Egypt, a great deal of time was spent in preparing the pharaoh for the mummification process upon his death. The pyramid would be for his burial. One of two parts of the soul, the "ka," considered to be the spiritual essence and double of the pharaoh's god-given powers, would travel the afterlife in other dimensions. If the pharaoh had accomplished a good life, then he would care well for the country and be reborn as Ra, the sun god.

According to the Egyptians, the other part of the soul, the "ba," the personality essence, remained in the physical dimension connected with the body and able to travel in and out of the body's tomb.

The ancient history mixed with the modern city of Cairo represents the mystique that is still vibrant and very much alive in Egypt. The energy is strong inside of the pyramids. The pictures on the inside walls show the energy of Ra coming into the pyramid to the pharaoh, and the hieroglyphics pray for the pharaoh to still be of service to his people in the afterlife.

Hermes Thrice-Great Trismegistus lived three lives in Egypt starting with Thoth Hermes who lived his first life as an expression of the sun god, bringing the *Emerald Tablet* to us over ten thousand years ago. He brought us Hermetic

Philosophy, which is found in the Gnostic Gospels and was the forerunner of what we now call alchemy. He was responsible for the invention of hieroglyphics and writing ideas for organizing speech for communication. He was concerned with consciousness and the soul of humanity. The Egyptians knew Him as God.

Hermes' second life was as Pharaoh Amenhotep IV, eventually changing his name to Akhenaten and bringing the country to worship one God, the sun god called "The Disk." This is the "All That Is." This is also the Mind of God, which is the source of everything of all creation. He instilled the concept of living in truth. The reign of Akhenaten was from 1351 BCE to 1334 BCE, seventeen years, ending with his disappearance.

Hermes' third life was as a poor healer named Balinas around 64 BCE. During this particular lifetime, he re-discovered the *Emerald Tablet*. Written on it were the words: "Behold, I am Hermes Trismegistus, he who is threefold in wisdom." This refers to the masculine expression, the feminine expression, and the expression of pure Spirit.

My previous two books go into much more detail and explanation of Hermes' lives in Egypt.

Egypt's pyramids were considered power centers and sometimes used as burial temples where prayer was offered to raise the vibration of the pharaohs for admission to Maat in the heavens. Even after death, the pharaoh's role was to continue looking after his people.

The worship included meditation and healing, and the Wisdom and Love rays upon migration to Egypt.

Angkor Wat

The Hindu religion is the oldest formal religion we can verify in the world, being ten thousand years old, but over the centuries it has undergone constant change and transformation.

The temple complex at Angkor Wat is located northwest from the center of Cambodia and is the largest religious monument in the world. The original name means the "Sacred Dwelling of Vishnu." It was built in the early 1100s as a temple dedicated to the Hindu God Vishnu and changed to a Buddhist temple in the late 1100s. It is now referred to as a Hindu-Buddhist temple and is surrounded by a three-mile-long moat.

Angkor Wat is the Capitol of the Khmer Empire. The temple-mountain is designed to represent Mount Meru, home of the devas in Hindu mythology, with three raised rectangular galleries, each raised above the other. Angkor Wat has become a symbol for Cambodia, appearing on the national flag.

There are three parts to God or Trinity that the Hindus call the Trimurti. Brahma is the first part as creator of the Universe. Vishnu is the second part as preserver and protector of the Universe. Shiva is the third part as the destroyer.

Vishnu has gained prominence as the most holy. He is believed to have reincarnated many times—the most important being "Krishna" as spoken of in the Bhagavad-Gita. Lord Vishnu is Hindu's savior and peace-loving God. He sustains the principles of order, righteousness, and truth. When these values are threatened, Vishnu rises to restore peace and order, returning afterward to a state of transcendence. Vishnu brings harmony and balance. Like Brahma, he creates. And like Shiva, he destroys. He includes the wisdom to combine the head and the heart, keeping sight of the big picture.

Vishnu relates to the energies of the Sun and to Light, and espouses the virtues of truth and peace in empowerment. He rides the Garuda eagle, spreading the knowledge of the Vedas.

Both Hindu and Buddhist worship include discipline and meditation, as well as fearless devotion under stressful situations.

Vishnu is accompanied by many colorful demigods, most of them taking the form of animals. The ten Earthly incarnations of Vishnu are Matsyavatara the fish, Koorma the tortoise, Varaaha the boar, Narasimha the man-lion, Vamana the dwarf, Parasurama the angry man, Lord Rama the perfect human of the Ramayana, Lord Balarama Krishna's brother, Lord Krishna divine diplomat and statesman, and awaiting the tenth incarnation as Kalki Avatar.

Vishnu appears with blue transparent skin and has four hands, a conch on the back of one representing OM, the sound of creation. In another hand, he has a chakra or discus representing the mind. In yet another hand, he has a lotus flower representing a glorious existence and liberation. In the fourth hand, he holds a mace representing mental and physical strength. His consort is Lakshmi standing in a lotus and representative of wealth, beauty, and abundance.

The Khmer empire built many temples and monuments to celebrate the divine authority of the Khmer kings. Hindu priests, called Brahmins, performed Hindu ceremonies and rituals only among the ruling elites. There is a theory that a plague wiped out the people in the 1300s. They left behind almost no written record of their society, so it is difficult to know what day-to-day worship the lower-class participated in before Buddhism became the main focus of religious practice in Angkor Wat.

Hindu and Buddhist religions have evolved from the early Wisdom and Love rays bringing grace and raising vibrations through chants and song.

Stonehenge

Stonehenge is a prehistoric site and religious monument located in Wiltshire, England. It consists of a ring of standing pillars of bluestone, each standing thirteen feet high and seven feet wide and weighing about twenty-five tons each. It is believed to have been built between 3000 BCE and 2500 BCE and was used as a cremation burial ground for the first five hundred years—bone remains have been found at the site.

The bluestones were believed to be quarried from a location in Wales, one hundred fifty miles away. The columns may have been transported on a series of logs tied together. This feat still boggles the mind.

It has been suggested that the area around Durrington Walls Henge was a place for the living. Stonehenge, on the other hand, was a place for the dead.

The design includes religious, mystical, and spiritual elements. It serves as a celestial observatory for prediction of events important to the religion of the times, such as an eclipse, solstice, equinox, etc. It was probably built as a symbol for peace and unity to go along with Britain's cultural unification.

The igneous bluestone possesses unusual acoustic properties. When struck, it responds with a loud clanging noise. Perhaps the reason it was transported so many miles to the site was because of the rarified energies emitted from the horseshoe monument opening to the northeast. It is still thought to be a sacred place of healing rituals and meditation.

In Wales, the town of Maenclochog—which means "ringing rock"—used the bluestones as church bells up to the late 1700s.

The Latin translation from the Celts describe the Druids as a social class who concerned themselves with prophesy and ritual. Since the Ancient Celts didn't use the written word, all accounts of the Druids have come from outside their culture.

Around 50 BCE, after Rome invaded France, which was then called Gaul, Julius Caesar wrote, "The Druids are engaged in things sacred, conduct the public and private sacrifices, and interpret all matters of religion." They had an interest in astrology, education, and valor, and a habit of using large wicker figures filled with live men and set on fire as a sacrifice to please the gods.

A Roman writer, Pliny the Elder, said that the Druids would hold rituals with mistletoe and human sacrifice. To murder a man was the highest act of devoutness. To eat his flesh was to gain the blessings for his own health. Tacitus described a battle in Wales where the Druids covered their altars with the blood of captives.

The issue of the gruesome rituals resurfaced in 1984 with the discovery of the two-thousand-year-old human remains in a bog in Cheshire England. The body that archeologists named Lindow Man had been preserved in the bog after suffering head blows and being stabbed and strangled centuries ago. They found mistletoe pollen in his stomach, leading to the question of whether his death came as a result of ritual sacrifice.

Mention of the Druids in medieval literature has come up many times with regards to their reputation for savagery and the fact that despite the Roman capture of many Celts in battle, the Romans were most afraid of going up against the Druids.

We have no knowledge of the time that Stonehenge was built, and very little is known about the culture and lifestyles of the Druids. However, since the time of Stonehenge, the Druid culture has become known for the Priests, the religion of old, and magic. Both the culture and the religion have evolved from the root rays of Power. Early culture emphasized war and sacrifice, but has grown to emphasize meditation, magic, and beauty.

We can surmise that their original focus was on Power and Wisdom with emphasis on beauty and magic in life.

Machu Picchu

Machu Picchu, a fifteenth century Inca settlement in southern Peru with an elevation of 7970 feet, was discovered in 1911. This sacred place represents the origin of the Inca civilization. It is located fifty miles northwest of Cuzco and is protected by access of narrow trails and tropical mountain climate. At one time, it housed more than two hundred residents. Besides the drystone walls for the residences, it has three main structures—the *Intihuatana*, the *Temple of the Sun*, and the *Room of the Three Windows*. The Intihuatana was the highest point. The buildings had been thirty percent restored by 1976.

It is believed that Machu Picchu was built to honor two rulers—Pachacutec Inca Yupanqui who ruled from 1438 to 1471, and Tu'pac Inca Yupanqui who ruled from 1472 to 1494. It was used for eighty years and abandoned, along with several other Inca settlements, at the time of the Spanish conquests.

INTIHUATANA

*M*achu Picchu's Intihuatana was carved from a huge slab of rock, standing high above the Sacred Plaza. Tiered with a small rock needle at the top, it is thought to connect the different levels of the Inca mythology—Spiritual World, Now, and Underworld—in one focal point.

The four sides of the Intihuatana represent the four cardinal directions—north, south, east, and west. Ceremonies performed there were meant to hold the sun in place, ensuring a good harvest and general prosperity. The Winter Solstice festival is known as Inti Raymi, and is still being celebrated in Cusco each year. The periods of the equinoxes were determined by the shadows and light as they interacted with the pillars accordingly.

TEMPLE OF THE SUN

*I*nca natives held sacred ceremonies on the summer and winter solstices to give offerings to the sun. The sun was considered to be responsible for the creation of all things. Only sacred priests were allowed inside the Temple of the Sun. In the center of the Temple of the Sun is a large altar carved from rock, where the ceremonies and sacrifices would have been performed. The vertical alignment was designed to bring in the light from above. Underneath the temple is a cave believed to have been the burial site of Pachacutec.

TEMPLE OF THE THREE WINDOWS

*T*he Temple of the Three Windows was built up with the purpose to hide the Inca civilization from the Spanish conquerors.

The Temple of the Three Windows still retains the names of the builders engraved in stone. This attests to the history of the culture. This building is among the most important of

Machu Picchu because of its close location on the eastern part of the main Plaza.

Consisting of only three walls on a rectangular base, and covered by a roof made of adobe walls, the temple was constructed from large blocks of solid rock carved in polygonal shape. Originally, it had five windows, but today only three of them are left. They indicate the location of the sunrise. The roof is supported by a column of stone with engravings that represent the three levels where the Inca civilization divided the Andean world: Sky spirituality is called "Hanan-Pacha," Earth is called "Kay-Pacha," and the underworld is called "Ukju-Pacha."

Most everyone who enters the settlement of Machu Picchu can feel the higher consciousness of the energies of the natural vortex. My good friend Anne, who made a spiritual quest to Machu Picchu, shared that she had a guide and was with a group on a spiritual adventure. They were all climbing the steep and narrow path to get to the top. Along the way, she slipped and started to fall backward. Someone behind her caught her and pushed her forward. When she got a chance to look back to say thanks, there was no one there behind her.

This gives us some idea of the high spiritual energies and the benevolent spirit beings there to help us on our discoveries. Their focus was seemingly on Power, Love, and Wisdom.

The Vatican

The official name for the Vatican is the "Holy See." It is an independent city-state within Rome, Italy, and the seat of the Catholic Church. Vatican City was created by the Laf Treaty in 1929 establishing it as a sovereign territory with full ownership and exclusive dominion. It is a separate country with a separate government within Rome. When necessary, the Holy See will make treaties on behalf of Vatican City.

It is a religious state with medieval walls on all sides, except on the southeast boundary, which opens onto Saint Peters Square. It is one hundred and ten acres and includes the world's largest church, Saint Peter's Basilica, as well as the Sistine Chapel and Michelangelo's Pieta.

There has been a backstory behind the Vatican that is shrouded by mystery and intrigue. It involves the *Prophesy of the Popes*. In 1139 AD, Saint Malachy received inspiration naming the succession of Popes to come in the future. It was published in 1595 AD. All the prophesy was correct for each Pope up to Pope Benedict.

Pope Benedict announced on February 11, 2013, that due to his age and health, he was stepping down from his post as Pope. Six hours later, lightning struck the peak of Saint Peter's Basilica, not once, but twice. Pope Benedict officially resigned on February 28, 2013.

The prophesy of Saint Malachy did not foresee the resignation of Pope Benedict, only that the Pope to follow Pope Benedict would be "Petrus Romanus"—Peter the Roman. The Prophesy stated that the successor to Pope Benedict would be the last Pope and that he would be followed by the tribulation.

The new Pope was selected in March of 2013, but instead of taking the name of Benedict or Petrus Romanus, the new Pope chose the name of "Pope Frances." Perhaps the resignation of Pope Benedict and the name selection of Pope Frances were designed in an attempt to break the chain of events in prophesy. The final chapters of the *Prophesy of the Popes* will soon be played out in the near future for us all to see in our lifetime.

Catholicism is, at present, the second largest religion in the world. The sacred texts include the fundamentals of Catholicism, the Catechism, plus the Code of Canon Law.

This provides formal prayer structure to the masses. Frequent prayer brings us closer to God.

THE LORD'S PRAYER (Aramaic translation)

Father in heaven, Sanctified be thy Name. Let thy Kingdom come. Let thy Will be done, as above so upon Earth. Keep giving us the bread (*teaching*) we need from day to day, and forgive us our debts (*sins*) as we also forgive everyone indebted to us. Let us not enter into the test (*wrongful thinking*), but deliver us from evil (*wickedness, mistake*) for Thine is the Kingdom and the Power and the Glory forever and ever.

Amen, Amen, and Amen.

GLORY BE

Glory be to the Father, and to the Son, and to the Holy Spirit; as it was in the beginning, is now, and ever shall be, world without end.

Amen, Amen, and Amen.

HAIL MARY

Hail Mary, full of grace, the Lord is with thee! Blessed art thou amongst women, blessed is the fruit of thy womb, Jesus. Holy Mary, Mother of God, pray for us now, the hour of our death, and forever.

Amen, Amen, and Amen.

APOSTLE'S CREED

I believe in one God, the Father Almighty, Creator of Heaven and Earth; and in Jesus Christ, His only son, our Lord; who was conceived by the Holy Spirit, born of the Virgin Mary, suffered under Pontius Pilate, was crucified, died and was buried. He descended into hell. On the third day, He rose again from the dead. He ascended into Heaven, and sitteth at the right hand of God, the Father Almighty. From thence shall He come to judge the living and the dead. I believe in one God. I believe in the Holy Spirit. I believe in miracles. I believe my prayers are heard and answered. I believe in the communion of saints, the forgiveness of sins, the resurrection of the body, and life everlasting through the Sacred Heart of Jesus Christ, the Holy Spirit of God and Mary Mother of our Lord and Savior, Mary Queen of peace.

Amen, Amen, and Amen

DEVOTION OF THE ROSARY

1) Holding the Crucifix, make the sign of the cross, saying, "In the name of the Father, Son, and the Holy Spirit." Then say the Apostle's Creed.

2) The Lord's Prayer is said with the first bead above the cross.

3) Hail Mary is said one at a time for the next three beads.

4) Glory be is to be said on the chain after the previous three beads.

5) The Lord's Prayer is said on the following bead.

6) Hail Mary is said on the first set of ten beads of the rosary, say the Hail Mary one time for each bead.

7) Glory be and the Lord's Prayer are both said on the next bead.

8) Hail Mary is said on each bead for the second set of ten beads.

9) Glory be and the Lord's Prayer are both said on the next bead.

10) Hail Mary is said on each bead on the third set of ten beads.

11) Glory be and the Lord's Prayer are both said on the next bead.

12) Hail Mary is said on each bead on the fourth set of ten beads.

13) Glory be and the Lord's Prayer are both said on the next bead.

14) Hail Mary is said on each bead on the fifth set of ten beads.

15) Glory be and the Lord's Prayer are both said on the last bead to close.

The Catholic tradition has been known through history to maintain discipline (Power), Wisdom, Love, and firm adherence to the prayers and ceremonies of old that have been carried forward to Europe.

The Hathor Temple

Napoléon led an army through an area sixty miles north of Luxor, on the Nile River, in December of 1798. It was there they discovered an ancient temple known as the Temple of the Goddess Hathor—a historic archeological find that changed the world view about the beginnings of Egypt. On the ceiling in an upstairs room, was a discovery of the Dendera Zodiac. Depicted were constellations representing twelve houses spiraling inward in a circular astrological configuration, with the first house being Cancer. These and other artifacts made it clear the ancient people who once lived there worshipped Enki, the ancient Sumerian God of the waters, and Utu, the ancient Sumerian Sun God.

The temple walls were decorated with art, statues, and hieroglyphics in service to the Light, to keep ancient spiritual teachings alive. Inspiration, healing, and protection were instilled in the temple, with Light and kundalini energies being channeled through Goddess Hathor for initiations and the benefit of humankind.

According to the hieroglyphics found there, the original temple was built in the year 8000 BCE, although it underwent further renovation at a later date. The symbols referenced civilization as far back as 14000 BCE. The only known civilization that goes back that far is the civilization of Atlantis.

The Temple of Hathor was aligned with the ancient stars in the sky. It was aligned with the constellation of the Great Bear, which was unusual in comparison to alignment of other ancient sites of newer construction.

The writing makes reference to a major infusion of Light energies from the Pleaides constellation streaming down to Goddess Hathor, and mentions the Seven Sisters of the Pleaides energetically assisting humankind. This influx of energy is still with us today, providing healing and a buoyancy-bubble of electromagnetic field to provide protection and sacred assistance, shielding our progress of evolution. The electromagnetic field is so strong that it's said to affect our ability to walk. Its effect on cameras and computer equipment is also noticeable.

This knowledge has come forward in history with the ability of humankind to translate the hieroglyphics now opening up to us since the time of its discovery.

The upper chamber of the temple has twelve very tall granite pillars inscribed with hieroglyphics and infused with Light and sound encoded to hold a sacred space within the temple.

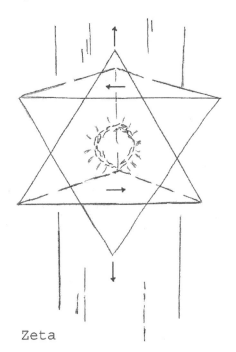

Zeta

There are two very important bits of information that have come forward to us concerning all ancient matter, energy, and sound vibration that were used in the temple. The first was a machine with energies spinning in opposite directions. This was called a Zeda machine —pronounced with a long ē. With counter rotating energies, an electromagnetic field of subtle energies was created and installed at the ceiling and into the pillars as Light and sound flowed into the temple.

The second important bit of information was a strong hand-held tool that was used. It had a handle with the symbolic face of the Goddess Hathor on top. A long loop extended above her face. The tool was called a sistrum, and was used for activating a connection through prayer and intention, invoking the Goddess Hathor, and tying into subtle but strong kundalini energies for rejuvenation. These energies flow down from God and the Pleaides for protection and healing, and anchor to Mother Earth to complete the flow of electromagnetic energy.

The ancient technology of Light includes a balance in numerology of 144 in matter, 144 in energy, and 144 in sound vibration, adding up to 432 (which is the perfect vibration to resonate with the heart of Goddess Hathor) and transcends Earth's polarity of masculine and feminine, thereby uplifting our spiritual essence.

The twelve houses and their constellations give us input of consciousness that we must move through and experience in order to incarnate on Earth.

The face of Goddess Hathor is facing the four elements and four sacred directions transcending time and space. The feminine nature and polarity of beingness with Spirit was brought from Atlantis into the world to balance the rampant expression of masculine energies that have been misqualified, ego-driven, and used to dominate finance, commerce, authority, and religion.

In ancient Egyptian culture, the Goddess Hathor was known as a great Mother energy, giving the feminine aspect a somewhat different role than that of modern times. Goddess Hathor is pictured on many Egyptian temples honoring her, as well as in statues and in the temple which bears her name. Her face in the Hathor Temple, and elsewhere, is wide with the big eyes and long protruding ears of a cow—symbolic of the feminine role and warm, loving energies streaming to us in nurturing, teaching, and protecting humankind with Sacred Light. This is much the same as bringing milk and cream to nurture humankind with the support of life and rejuvenation. The vast star system known as the "Milky Way" was named after these energies.

The Hathors focus was on Power derived from Wisdom and Love, with emphasis on nourishing and nurturing humanity.

Overview

These many ancient religions have laid the foundations for the religions and political movements of today. The energies of Wisdom and Love and Power that have affected the World throughout history are still with us, shaping our growth and transformation. In addition, there are other power spots yet to be discovered and investigated for ourselves.

As spirits having a human experience, it is our nature to want to control our circumstances and environment, and share in prayers during difficult times, as well as celebrate in times of good fortune. We gather to combine our energies in prayer. All prayer works to raise humanity to higher consciousness.

It is up to us to work individually to raise our vibrations in order to contribute this higher vibration on a higher frequency to all group connections with God most High. Direct connection with God requires no middleman. Religion can assist us to reaching a higher vibration, while at the same time, we bring our individual connection with God to our religious groups.

Self-discovery is our aim for our own spiritual growth and evolution!

Throughout time, there have been great forces of Light shining into darkness. Religions of all shapes and sizes have had to endure the battle between them through political and power struggles within and without, just as happens for each of us individually as we struggle to reconcile the dark and Light in our own inner and outer worlds in our own lives. The Light reveals and dissolves all darkness. Dark forces have brought some pretty bleak times in the history of humankind, yet our strength is always in being solid in our truth, our faith, and our alignment with Light, living in prayer.

NO MATTER HOW DEEP THE DARKNESS GOES,

DEEPER STILL IS THE LIGHT!

The Qabalah wisdom teaches the infusion of Light to planet Earth and to humanity. If the Light is misqualified to focus on a dark, manipulative use of the energy, then it is up to each of us to use centering and grounding alignment within ourselves, through highest alignment dimensions back to Mind, Source God. We bring Light back down in prayer, infusing higher Light into ourselves, for our good health and prosperity, and blessing humanity, blessing our leaders.

We are holding a focus in the Light. We release fear and insecurities to the Light, bringing alignment with Christ Holy Spirit and our soul, with our truth of Light within. We bring stability to our energy field with alignment in single focus and empowerment through the Light and our truth, and single expression of our Sacred Space with Holy Spirit.

We always release our challenges in family, social, economic, and political dissention of the world into the Light. Connecting with higher dimensions of Light in prayer brings the influence of higher Love, compassion, wisdom and grace to dissolve controversy and violence.

"Beware of false prophets, who come to you in sheep's clothing, but inwardly they are ravenous wolves."
- Yahushua, Matthew 7:15 NKJV

Lord,
Give us eyes to see,
Give us ears to hear,
Give us discernment of spirit to know the truth,
We stand in perfect alignment with Light,
We pray for Love and Light to prevail!
Amen, Amen, and Amen

"Our personal growth in consciousness
adds to the growth in group consciousness."

- John Pollock

CHAPTER III — THE HATHORS

Hathor was a major goddess, worshipped from 8000 BCE up until 2650 BCE in ancient Egypt, at which point Isis came into prominence. Hathor is mentioned in many temples of old throughout Egypt. She was the consort of the Sky God Horus and the Sun God Ra, and the symbolic mother of the pharaohs. She is also known as the Goddess of Love.

Hathor was the feminine counterpart to the Eye of Ra, providing sacred protection, on the one hand, and benevolent expression of music, dance, joy, love, sexuality, and maternal care, on the other. These two aspects were the embodiment of all feminine energy and expression. Hathor extended consciousness into Higher realms and assisted souls of the departed in crossing over to Spirit.

Major information has come in meditation to Tom Kenyon and Virginia Essene during the mid to late 1980s. Through them, the Hathors tell us that they might be termed an "ascended civilization." They have been in a process of evolution much like the planet Earth. They have grown from experience, as we all share our common expression of Love.

The Hathors came to share the vision of a "dream reality" for Earth. They describe their own nature as energetic and interdimensional, working with sacred geometry and sound. All civilizations are growing and changing, some being further along than others, some having reached advanced wisdom and vibration. It is said that we are all teachers and we are all students.

The Hathors tell us that they came to us through the star Sirius, a portal or entry point into our universe. They state that they bring a loving influence from etheric realms of Venus and work with Hathor, the fertility goddess of ancient Egypt. The Hathors shared information with the Tibetan lamas during the formative period of Tibetan Buddhism. They prayed alongside Sanat Kumara and the Ascended

Masters to raise consciousness and assist in evolution of planet Earth and our solar system.

They tell us that we are all part of the mystery, part of the love that holds and binds all of the universe together. The Hathors vibrate at a higher rate and operate at higher levels of consciousness. They continue to offer the benefits of their lessons. It is up to us to determine if these lessons ring true and are useful for us.

The Hathors come in love to remind us of this higher understanding and focus. Yet, we can get stuck in habits of uncaring disinterest and assume that something or someone else will magically transform us. This false belief is an illusion. The Hathors teach that we must each take responsibility for our own growth and make changes in ourselves. They claim that ascension requires mastery of self-awareness to raise all levels of our consciousness.

SPIRITUALITY IS AN INSIDE JOB!

The Hathors tell us that it is up to us to do the work for our own ascension and elevation. Though other spiritual beings may offer information and energetic support, they do not want to interfere with our spiritual guidance, relationships, or religious beliefs.

The Ascended Master Sanat Kumara was the one who asked the Hathors to enter this Universe. He has taken on responsibilities for the elevation of planet Earth and this solar system. He is working for ascension and the evolution of consciousness, and so are the Hathors.

We are told that the Hathors ascended together as a civilization numbering over a million people. After thirty years of healing and meditation work, I met with four members in a private home after a spiritual group meeting was over. The people had diverse backgrounds, and we were experimenting with different meditations when somehow the subject of the Hathors came up. I was telling everyone what I knew about the subject, which wasn't very much. Everyone was still caught up in spiritual energies from previously meditating in the first group, and the energies were still high. Suddenly, we all noticed the energies were going even higher, and we had the awareness that the Hathors had joined us. There were messages that night, but the most memorable for me was the intensity of the Loving energies.

The Goddess Hathor is the goddess of love, although not in the same sense that humankind would normally relate to it. Humanity normally relates to love relationships with a striving to find an attractive partner to which each person is drawn, and that each person has emotional chemistry that attracts them as a potential partner.

Goddess Hathor tells us that it would better serve us to look inside at the love we have for ourselves. It is the loving of ourselves that attracts loving partners to us. That is also where the personal issues await our processing and release work. Most issues need merely to be released to the light where our soul energies can dissolve them. The obsessive-compulsive form of processing very rarely solves problems, but only serves to build pressure on ourselves for resolution. It is up to each of us to honor ourselves and our relationship partners with understanding.

In the three-dimensional world here on Earth, relationships with a partner involve attraction with energy welling up and taking over in a strong purpose of romance and emotional chemistry. The energies arise from the Base chakra, Sacral chakra, Solar Plexus, and Heart chakra. Energies bring with them issues from the Earth plane including power and control, struggle, abandonment, rejection, betrayal, authority, success and failure, life and death, survival, and male and female issues of all kinds.

Perhaps relationship issues and attraction on Earth level serve a purpose for drawing humankind together through heart and bringing us closer to Spirit, connecting us to Source in higher dimensions.

Sex brings the energies of the kundalini upward, integrating with the higher chakras and continuing work in higher and higher realms to assist enlightenment.

In the physical world, there is often a split in energies perceived between the physical world and the spiritual realms. In Spirit there is such consciousness as integrity, one truth of higher unconditional Love, blessings for all, a win-win outcome, honoring all life as sacred expression.

Centering, grounding, and aligning with soul can be brought into romance, lifting up ourselves and our partner in higher Love. This brings a transcendental aspect to life and promotes integration of all those parts of separation.

In much the same manner, we turn over to God other issues from the Earth plane that are playing out in our lives. We pray to reach an altered state with Spirit, and at the same time, we put issues with authority, abandonment, struggle, support, self-esteem, self-confidence, and empowerment into the Light of higher consciousness and higher wisdom. The higher vibration helps us dissolve the charge on these issues, lifting up the essence of our truth and our energy field. We hold these issues up to higher light and watch for our advancement in vibration and awareness.

Abandonment encompasses loss of a loved one, including loss of a relationship partner. We can recognize the pain in our heart as an abandonment issue, and fill the hole in our heart with our self and with Light. We may have lost a loved one, but we are still whole and complete.

Empowerment includes success and the personal empowerment to attract miracles into our life through alignment with Spirit.

In addition to areas of romance, raising ourselves in higher Love involves lifting ourselves above the glamour of the physical world and being open to expansion of consciousness, greater wisdom, and enlightenment. Meditation takes us to an altered state where we can choose to ask for guidance and empowerment in alignment with Light. Here, the Light takes over with the Holy Spirit, and our soul's purpose, to show us a progression over time, in perfect timing toward our enlightenment.

Many men have polarity issues with women. Many women have polarity issues with men. In relationships, these polarity issues surface as feelings that repeatedly arise in certain situations. In these situations, both men and women feel diminished and unempowered from time to time. Certain things peculiar to ourselves and our individual experiences, replay in our lives. We are intimidated by our partner and feel overpowered from time to time. We may withdraw and give in to our partner when we don't think it's justified or fair from our perspective.

We always begin healing prayer by calling ourselves to center and ground and into alignment with Spirit. We call our truth forward from within our heart into perfect alignment with our soul and higher self, Divine Father and Mother God, to the purest heart of Love and Light of all creation and "All That Is." We call ourselves to connect to ground in nurturing and support, in balance with Spirit and the physical, and for empowerment through alignment with Light. We call forth the four cardinal directions to anchor the workings of higher light through us.

We remember situations where these issues are affecting us. We raise these experiences and put them into higher Light of soul, seeing and feeling the experiences explode in Light, feeling a strong clearing and empowerment of soul-purpose. We notice that the issues we are working with have ceased to affect us. Release of heavy issues, and sound in Tibetan bells or gongs, Lighten our essence for our process of ascension.

Hermes' information over ten thousand years ago, and applies every bit as much to the present, was concerned with humankind being caught up in Earth-level group karma. Hermes was concerned about our inability to balance shared karma to advance. What he saw was that humankind was getting bogged down and reliving the same group issues over and over

The ascension of the Hathor civilization gives us hope in lifting up humanity with a common goal of expressing love and grace in our lives, while also working diligently toward a path of ascension.

There are many diversions in the physical world, yet it is good to remember that our ultimate path is uniting us with our source, the All That Is!

Rendering of the Temple of Goddess Hathor

"As Light is infused to bolster our life expression,
we feel emotions and our connection to higher wisdom
and consciousness from Spirit."

- John Pollock

CHAPTER IV — THE ENERGETIC UNIVERSE

The Angels tell us that the best way to teach about the energies of humankind and the Universe is to start with the understanding we already have concerning the human chakra system.

The chakra system of the body is a system of stair-stepping consciousness and rising levels of energy vibration. Each level has a different function and a different purpose to support the different aspects of the physical, etheric cell memory, emotional makeup, and lower mental and rational thought. It also connects us to Spirit from Higher dimensions, bringing in energetic Light to support all life. This is our auric field that fills and encompasses the body.

I have discussed the chakra system at length in my previous two books, *Prayers for All Occasions* and *MYSTIC*. Just as the energies increase in vibration rate as they move from one level to another, so too, are the levels of the etheric and Spirit. Light, with differing vibration and levels of consciousness, travels between different levels of God consciousness for differing purposes.

The Base chakra holds the physical level energies supporting cells of the body, along with etheric cell memory that also connects to flows of the emotional body that is the second chakra. As Light is infused to bolster our life expression, we feel emotions and our connection to higher wisdom and consciousness from Spirit. It is from the second chakra that we make this connection to higher Light. We feel relationship issues often represent our power struggles verses the empowerment of our personhood. We also feel the powerful and sometimes Earth-shaking sexual energies associated with romance.

As energy moves from our Base chakra physical vitality and through our second chakra for success, it combines with heart energies of unconditional love and discernment flowing down through the solar plexus mental sensing and knowingness for safety, fight verses flight. The Holy Spirit flows through all levels in the body, from lower bodily functions to higher sensing and projection of higher guidance and grace, lifting us to higher awareness and deeper understanding of life.

As with the different levels of energies of Light working in the body, there are also a multitude of levels in the etheric. Each level has different purposes and different beings of Light in service to God. The Angels tell us there are a multitude of angels, not all in service to humankind, but all in service to God. Archangels Raphael, Michael, Gabriel, and Uriel are known to be in service to humanity. Some other teachers working with humanity during this time are Archangels Haniel, Ezekial, Tzadkiel, and Guardian Angel Romiel. Tzadkiel has joined us as the Violet transmuting flame that we've also known as the same Archangel from the TREE OF LIFE. Although having differing areas of service, all Archangels have one thing in common, they all come through great Love.

Each of the chakras has their own function and purpose, yet they are connected to each other. Energies in each chakra connect to the next through an energy portal or vortex that is focused in each chakra. Movement of energies up and down through the body helps us to stay balanced on many levels. We are multifaceted beings bringing levels of physicality and many levels of soul aspects together in balance and empowerment. It is the higher wisdom and consciousness from God and higher dimension that makes up our spiritual guidance and brings answers to our prayers.

Most lower functions of the body are regulated by automatic processes, but as we move to higher chakras and higher function, the energies are more and more responsive to our choice and intentions. For example, breathing is automatic, but we can purposely hold our breath if we want.

Using affirmation is based on being able to put forth our intentions for our self and having them carry through in our life. Using prayer brings higher realms and a deeper level of consciousness into play. At some point, our prayers involve asking for things that affect other people. This is the point where karmic consequences arise. Karma states that energy interchange with others will generate a return of energy in like nature. The Lords of Karma oversee this process. The universe is a sealed system, always moving to maintain an energetic balance.

In the case of dark thoughts and selfish desires, these wishes for others may work short-term, but sooner or later these wishes return to the original sender. In street jargon, "what goes around comes around." Likewise, if we live in Love and Light, we promote a win-win interaction, wishing a blessing for all. Blessings return the love we are putting out. Our life-lesson becomes how we can best express Love, teach Love, and be blessed. Our dance with life contains song and dance and joy.

What we learn about energy and Light gives us insight into the higher realms. Our prayers for miracles, for healing with permission, and for uplifting life experience—not to interfere with the free will of others—all begins with our intention. Our intention is released to the Light in prayer. It is the Light of God that brings everything into existence and through whom all blessings flow.

Our prayers to God are answered by Sacred prayer from God that brings things to manifest into creation and into existence. Sacred prayer from within God is the language of God. Our sincere and heartfelt prayer is our direct line to God.

We meditate often to raise the vibration of the essence of our being. The more we meditate, the easier it becomes to connect quickly with God. We begin to carry more Light. The blessings from God reflect Love and appreciation we have for God.

In higher dimensions, our connection with God brings our expansion of consciousness. This is truly a labor of Love! All beings are in service to God and His will is done.

Meditation, Prayer, and Invocation

I t is practical to prepare ourselves before we send our prayer. We must be receiving Light to prepare to send Light in service. We need to call our truth forward from within our heart, into perfect alignment with our Soul and Higher Self, Divine Father and Mother God, to the purest heart of Love and Light of all creation and All That Is.

We also call ourselves to ground in nurturing and support, in balance with the spirit and the physical, and in empowerment through Light.

We want to charge ourselves with Light in meditation before we begin. After prayer and healing work is finished, affirm that the work is done and complete. This is vital in order to release our prayer to the Light for completion through the energies of God and the Universe. Without releasing the prayer to go to work, it just sits with us without completing our intention.

Another matter is clarity of intention. A prayer works best without clouding the request with our own emotional issues. I had an occasion to have a vehicle stolen. After submitting a police report, I released a prayer to Spirit that I wanted my vehicle back but that I didn't necessarily need to catch the culprits. Shortly thereafter, the vehicle was found, taken to the county impound lot, and returned to me. Thank you, God.

The final thing to know about prayer is that sincerity and openness, as well as a desire to receive on the part of the recipient, are more important than the fame of a good facilitator. Many times, I have gone to an event thinking and praying that I needed to have a healing from a particular well-known individual. Upon leaving, I realized my prayers were actually unexpectedly answered by someone else, someone that I had not anticipated.

Channeled Energies

Channeling is a phenomenon to understand about energies of the Light. We use our intention to call our chakras into alignment with our truth within our heart, with ground, and with soul. We can visualize all the chakras coming into alignment in a straight line as the Light comes down through us. Light anchors into Mother Earth.

When the central focus of the chakra vortex energies has become aligned, energies of one vortex level are then compatible with energies of the next vortex level. Likewise, we call ourselves into alignment with Soul and Higher Self, Father and Mother God, to the purest heart of Love and

Light, and All That Is. We are calling ourselves into alignment with higher and higher levels within God, to Mind, the very source of All That Is!

Light then descends through this alignment, or "channel," down through our chakras to Mother Earth. This is not unlike electricity running from a battery through an appliance, then to ground. Instead of wiring, however, all that is required is purity of heart to be compatible with God's Love, and visualization to infuse Light. The Light vibrates through us like the feeling of water flowing through a water hose. Light follows our intention to send blessings, and then to ground to manifest them into physical reality.

In higher dimensions, the energies of God act according to our intention to align with the Higher Love of the Universe and to act in accordance with the purpose of the Holy Spirit. A sacred altar would be an example of such an alignment. Our intention to hold a sacred connection to the Light would maintain that connection *and* maintain the sacred purpose for ourselves and others, providing empowerment and freedom in the highest and best interest of ALL, and not to interfere with free will.

Understanding alignment of energies of the body with higher levels of Light extending to Source "All That Is" helps us to see energies in motion as they move from one point to another. On one occasion, several energy workers, including myself, were invited to appear as guests on a radio show. We opened the show to questions from the radio audience. One caller requested a healing. We said a prayer and sent Light for healing. An interesting thing happened for me. In my Third-Eye chakra, I had a vision with Spirit of gold lines fanning out from each person on the panel. I was then directed to energetically draw all the lines being sent back to focus on the person asking for the healing. I had no idea that any such thing could happen. It was clear to me that Spirit was working through me for the healing. It was a teaching lesson for me.

Prayer Ritual Reaching Higher

A Ritual Prayer creates an energetic bubble for one or more persons to unite with beings of the light in sacred prayer for spiritual purpose. It is usually more formal and involves a fire or candle in the center of a prayer circle with an invocation of the Sacred Four Directions to come forward from outside of us and join us in the center circle, turning downward into Mother Earth. The Sacred Four Directions are also the Four Sacred Elements. Air comes from the East, Fire comes from the South, Water comes from the West, Earth comes from the North. There is a flow outside of us forming a horizontal prayer circle and closing the circle around us. The energies move in a clockwise direction, forming a vortex of energies for prayer, for healing, or for meditation.

The four directions are joined by a flow from Father Sky above, through us to Mother Earth below. This is a vertical line that also flows upward through us from Mother Earth, returning to Father Sky. The leader of the ritual holds a sacred heart connection with all flows within the vortex. To the Native American Indians, this is known as a Medicine Wheel, using a Sacred Pipe in ceremony or being used in a Sacred Sweat Lodge.

Ritual prayer can be used quite successfully in times of crisis or great need. It uses more beings of Light to add to the prayer.

The Universe is made up entirely of energy, formed and unformed, always alive and carrying our prayers in vibration to higher or lower frequencies, depending on our intention and focus.

"By being solid in our resolve to see the best potential in life, things tend to go better."

- John Pollock

CHAPTER V — MAINTAINING A SINGLE FOCUS OF LOVE

The Universe has a myriad of flows moving upward and downward, from greater consciousness to lesser consciousness and back. At every level in the ethers there are Angels and Light Beings of service to God. Some are also in service to Humankind.

Prayer is what makes our connection with Spirit and drives our lives. The Love in our hearts is a silent prayer. It puts our intention out to the Universe regarding what things we want to have happen in the physical plane, in relationships, in business, in the national and world arenas, and in our spiritual path—in grace for all.

Making a connection in prayer with Spirit enables us to be blessed, to infuse Light for empowerment of ourselves. We bless and empower others to empower themselves. We pray for help to resolve situations and to bless other people. Our Prayers are for freedom and healing in their lives, but not to control the answers and outcomes of their challenges. A blessing of Love always lifts everyone to the highest level possible. Our prayers for others are that they will find the answers for their own challenges in the highest and best interest of everyone involved.

Our prayers to God ask for answers and blessings in our lives and the lives of others. God answers our prayers with His own prayers for us. His prayers for us are in the language of Light. When God speaks, He speaks everything into existence. We are blessed! Our prayers are answered. To the extent that our prayers align with the purpose of the Holy Spirit, our answers are forthcoming.

Love includes synchronicities in life's flow and achieving success with Spirit's priorities. We focus past seeing the half-empty glass. If we see the worst happening, many times we are inadvertently "creating" the worst possibilities. By being solid in our resolve to see the best potential in life, things tend to go better.

THERE IS AN ANSWER FOR EVERY QUESTION.
ASK SPIRIT FOR HELP!

Love includes higher possibilities and is always expanding the many ways of expressing the Love and Light flowing through us. There are always other choices, but having a single focus of Love involves consciously honoring ourselves. We make choices that are nurturing and self-supporting for our highest and best good, and for the good of all. A win-win attitude lifts consciousness in everyone.

A single focus of Love in our being is what Hermes speaks of as meditating to experience living in soul. He refers to that as having our own Philosopher's Stone to guide our life. The Philosopher's Stone is a mindset that can be taken anywhere and is always available.

In *Prayers for All Occasions,* we bring prayer and the invocation of Light into our lives. Praying often has the effect of raising consciousness and our vibration. We carry more Light, and as a result, we experience more grace and synchronicity in our lives.

In *MYSTIC,* we use the techniques we have learned to align our chakras with our soul and higher levels of Spirit. This enables us to begin living in our own soul and in alignment with higher spiritual guidance. We transcend the issues that generally affect humanity.

We already know that, at times, we in humanity have issues that come up to be addressed. When we look closely, we may see that we have generated many personal issues during this lifetime that challenge us to feel and release. Shared issues that affect humanity have yet to be resolved. Prayers for peace on a large scale are necessary to release cultural bias and considerable judgment.

What does a person have to do to begin living in soul? This question is discussed in-depth in *MYSTIC: Manifesting Your Soul, Truth in Consciousness.* Living in soul involves techniques to flash-burn and purify our essence, traveling in spiritual imagination to the Mind of God. We bring fire energies down from Mind, Source God, to help create the miracles in our lives and live in higher vibration. Mind combines with the ONE THING spoken of by Hermes in the *Emerald Tablet* to produce miracles.

How did a civilization like the Hathors teach ascension, let alone, get such a large group of people to all ascend together? We know there was a Temple to the Goddess Hathor in Egypt. Hathor was a consort and protective partner for Sky God Horus and Sun God Ra. She was the symbolic mother of the pharaohs and combined protection and nurturing. Meditation was undoubtedly a big key in lifting the energies of the Hathors to the place where they could ascend.

A big question for modern civilization is how everyone can ascend when so many are distracted with the glamor, success, and intrigue of the physical world. Hermes says that so many lose focus by losing sight of our spiritual purpose to learn from our experiences, to carry out our inner reflection in meditation, and to raise our consciousness in evolution.

ACCEPTANCE OF NOURISHMENT, LOVE, AND LIGHT GOES FURTHER IN LIFTING OUR SPIRITUAL ESSENCE THAN STRIVING TO ACCOMPLISH PLATITUDES OF ENLIGHTENMENT FORCED UPON US.

Our reference to single focus of Love has to do with our personal relationship with God. Not everyone has the same relationship with God, or the same kind of relationship that we have with ourselves, for that matter!

The spark of Light that burns within gives life to all of humankind, and is the means for life expression. White Light moves upward and downward, enabling cells of the body and consciousness at different levels of chakras to communicate with each other in their own language. This process is overseen by the White Ray of Archangel Gabriel. The Holy Spirit communicates with our soul and guides both our soul expression and our life's journey.

The Angels tell us that the Light is structured in different levels above, just as the chakras of the body are structured in different levels within the body, each having a different purpose and vibration.

With the help of guidance and in making a choice to follow a path of spiritual growth, we use the spiritual tools that we have been given. We meditate and pray. We bring in grace and self-mastery. We accept blessings and we wish to be of service as we may be guided. We align our Heart with Soul, Higher Self, and "All That Is."

We maintain a focus on the Highest. We infuse Light to charge our lives with a straight line of flow from on High above, through us, and anchoring below us to Mother Earth. Frequent meditation lifts us to an altered state where we lose track of time. This has a tendency to raise our lives into a state of grace.

Positive expectations, positive thoughts, and positive emotions all have a tendency to stabilize our lives and assist us to reach new potential. Negative expectations, such as doubts and fears, have a tendency to destabilize our lives and attract chaos. Fluctuation between putting out positive energies of prayer and then fighting against negative energies has a tendency to bring roller coaster drama into our life-experiences. Holding positive energies and positive expectations in prayer takes us on a journey of living in soul.

All thoughts are contained in Mind above. All emotions are contained in the ONE THING below. When Light from above is brought down to combine with emotions from below, miracles occur. "As above, so below" refers to higher realms of God—not to be confused with Heaven and Earth, which is all contained in the ONE THING along with all creation in the physical plane. This positive mindset with soul is known as our Philosopher's Stone.

In the second embodiment of Hermes Thrice-Great Trismegistus, born Amenhotep IV, he had a marked influence on the world in a short twenty-two-year reign. He changed his name to Akhenaten and changed worship in Egypt to the One God Aten, which was also known as the Sun God, or "The Disk." He stopped the polytheistic worship of many Gods. The outcome was a worship of Source God, the "Mind of God," or the Highest of God—the "All That Is."

It was during that time that Goddess Hathor was influenced to prayer with the one Source God, the "All That Is." The single focus of Love comes back to meditating with the one true God, the "Mind of God," the "All That Is."

Alignment with the ONE THING charges and guides our expression on the Earth plane, empowering us at soul level. We are guided past obstacles and our expression is lifted up.

The message is clear:

Be persistent—center, ground, and align often with Spirit in the present moment to know sweet integration of Love, Light, peace, support, and empowerment. We ask for help. Together with God, the blessings of Love and Light unfold in our Lives. Everyone must take responsibility to do their own work on themselves and with God. Spirituality is an inside Job! Do not waiver. Keep the faith. Keep the trust.

Namasté

"Everyone and everything are mirrors for us."

- John Pollock

CHAPTER VI — PRAYER, WHITE MAGIC & MIRRORS

It seems to us in the west that life is about learning to be a success in accumulating wealth and getting ahead, having a great family, and creating security with the outside world—being outer-directed for achievement.

Most of us have been chasing after outward signs of success but sometimes falling short of reaching the brass ring at the top. We are learning the valuable lessons that healthy competition provides—courage and perseverance to excel, to stretch and grow and discover our own personal inner strengths.

Feelings of inferiority and poverty consciousness are the "glass half empty" feelings that there is not enough to go around for everyone, so we think we must work harder to earn it or take it from others.

Buddhist and Hindu cultures have valued honoring ourselves, honoring others, lifting up consciousness for everyone, and being happy through inner direction. Meditation is used to access higher consciousness and growth. Sharing offers opportunity for all to achieve happiness. These cultures know the Light from within attracts and creates success and fulfillment.

We have already discussed aspects of prayer which add strength, clarity, and alignment with Spirit for empowerment. Technique only goes so far, however. It is then up to sincerity, charging our energy field with Love in our hearts, and maintaining a desire to be of service and to grow and expand with humankind. The journey for humanity involves everyone in diverse consciousness and understanding.

For those who use magic to create stronger energies, it is good to know that casting a spell is very much like invoking a strong prayer. In magical circles, white magic is used to send positive energies, not interfering with another's free will. Even wishing for what we think is best for someone else may be interfering with their choices. As a result, they may have to recreate their tests and lessons from their spiritual level. Both white magic and ritual invocation have a purpose to put a positive and beneficial spin on specific situations. We pray for freedom from issues and oppression, and for empowerment.

When energies are used to control another, or even attack another, the practice is considered dark magic. Dark magic is misusing energy and creating karmic debt that must be balanced somewhere down the road.

Prayer and white magic can both be used to send positive intention and package best wishes for a person's highest and best use. It is completely appropriate to direct a flow of Light to dark energies that are working through someone else in order to dissolve evil intent or attack.

Mirrors

Energies are constantly moving throughout the Universe, throughout all creation. As we begin to open up to our spiritual and energetic understanding of ourselves, we awaken to new philosophical and spiritual interaction with the Universe around us.

The mystic believes that humankind lives in a self-contained environment that constantly involves the laws of attraction and karma, proving that what we put out energetically returns to us. Our prayers are heard and answered by Spirit with the language of Light that puts a positive twist and a blessing on life experiences. Miracles can become commonplace if we are willing to receive and raise our vibration and expectations. We have faith and trust and look for more confirmation, always giving thanks to the Light. We take responsibility for creating our own lives, yet always turn our life-circumstances over to Spirit for higher guidance and direction. We ask for our needs to be met, planting seeds in prayer for blessings and guidance.

The Emerald Green flame of healing and truth, and the fine blessings of the Violet flame of transformation, combine with the Ruby and Gold flames of Christ energy of the Dove to heal and empower us. We give thanks!

The masters tell us that energies operating through others around us can be seen, felt, and understood by recognizing the dramas and adventures that are playing out around us. These "goings on" are mirrors of what energies we have inside and how they are getting projected into the Universe. The adventure and drama of others is drawn to us magnetically and reflects what is going on within ourselves.

Everyone and everything are mirrors for us. They show us what is happening outside of ourselves in life, and then we look within ourselves to discover where we are operating in much the same way. A good example of this might be when many other people appear to be angry or depressed and acting out their feelings as a reflection for us to see and to observe that our own mood could use some improvement.

As I get older, I find myself speaking louder to people so they will hear me and understand. Yet they seem to ignore me. Perhaps they feel that I think they are stupid and don't know what they are doing. That I feel like I'm not being heard in life is my own issue. When my issue is processed and released, the situation magically appears differently. When I change inside, the situation changes.

We can become aware of these situations in our lives. Our choice is to pay attention or to continue drawing the same circumstances to us. We can use these mirrors to see our issues more clearly and make a change in ourselves. Blaming others is to continue not taking responsibility for ourselves and keeps us in victim energy.

In years past, I journeyed to a nearby city to rent a booth at a fair and fulfill an opportunity to be of service. I would normally center, ground, and align myself in prayer at the start of a fair. I would ask for the clients I could benefit through Spirit, and money to pay for the venture. On that particular day, business was slow and I was wondering what was out of balance for me.

The issue for me was to accept empowerment and trust everything was in "right order" with Spirit, despite external appearances. Blaming people, the energies, or the time of year was only contributing to an unhappy afternoon. Spirit can only empower our energies when we are aligned with the purpose of Holy Spirit and in service to the Light. Sometimes our own issues must be dealt with before Spirit will let us proceed.

I once had a client, a single gentleman who had not been in a romantic relationship for over thirty years. He was in service as a facilitator for healing. He wasn't consciously aware that he was looking for a relationship. On one occasion, he met a woman who invited him to accompany her to a co-op food store. She called him several times and he felt that indicated the beginning of a "relationship." One day he called her to discuss how that "relationship" would proceed. After that conversation, she stopped returning his calls.

He felt heartache as though he had lost a true love. After thinking and meditating about the situation, he realized that he hadn't known her long enough or well enough to warrant his intense feeling of loss. Together, we realized the issue for him was "abandonment." She had raised his hopes by showing interest in him, then crushed his hopes by abruptly ending their contact. It was the issue of abandonment that was affecting him.

I suggested we get centered, grounded, and aligned with Spirit in meditation. We were guided to fill the hole in his heart with himself and with Spirit. He released the need for anything or anyone to make him whole or happy. The resolution was immediate—as soon as the prayer was done, the pangs of hurt subsided.

On a global scale, there has been ongoing social and political unrest, much war and strife, as well as earthquakes, fires, erupting volcanoes, tornadoes, hurricanes, and tsunamis around the world. These are some ways that Mother Earth responds to humanity's vibrations. When we infuse Light and meditate on what actions in Spirit would bring more peace, we can see healing things happening in humanity. The pandemic of 2020 spread around the world in record time. It seemed that risk of death was high, so schools, small businesses, sporting events, and other large gatherings and activities all shut down, giving everyone an opportunity to discover and recognize their own issues as they appeared on their own path.

Times of crisis provide us with mirrors to reflect what is happening in our inner world. We use the power of prayer to gain clarity about our inner issues and higher meaning. The outer world responds in a magical way.

Miracles happen when we recognize our inner truth and adjust in prayer accordingly.

"We can see the effect of Higher Light through the ultimate mirror — that of blessings, miracles, and grace flowing through our lives."

- John Pollock

Chapter VII — The Ultimate Mirror for Humanity

Mirrors are a tool to be used primarily on the Earth plane to see ourselves in the dramas and adventures that are playing out around us. What we see in others is their reality which has been created by them, but they have been drawn to us, magnetically, by our own energy field. Mirrors in the physical world also have influence from the beliefs of others, their motivation, group issues of humanity, and influence from Spirit. We can see the emotional baggage in others that we want to release in ourselves.

There is a different and greater mirror that reflects our creation by God, and gives us insight into our ascension process. His influence is expressing through our lives, lifting us up.

This mirror was given to us in the *Emerald Tablet,* written by Hermes Thrice-Great Trismegistus over ten thousand years ago and handed down in legend to Ancient Egypt and the known world. Hermes tells us in his own quest for truth, and among the other sources claiming to be in the know, that his inspiration came directly from the Mind of God and was the only source that he accepted as credible and coming from most High.

The most well-known teaching of the *Emerald Tablet* was "As Above So Below." The teaching tells us that the consciousness of Earthly expression is an extension of the Higher realms of God.

WE ARE GIVEN FREE WILL AND ARE EQUIPPED WITH
CREATIVITY, UNLIMITED POTENTIAL, AND INCREASED
EMPOWERMENT TO THE DEGREE THAT
WE ARE ALIGNED WITH SPIRIT.

We have freedom to make choices in life and freedom of self-discovery.

Each of us has a spark of Light within our heart which comes from God. That part of God deep inside allows everyone in humanity to connect to Spirit, to expand our consciousness, and to infuse Light into our lives. Our soul essence is raised up and we are Lighter. All we have to do is ask in prayer meditation and God knows the sincerity and desire in our heart. Our prayers are answered.

Humankind is empowered at birth by that spark of Light within, to attract life experience and to learn from the choices we make on our path. We also learn how to empower our life by aligning our chakras and our heart with our soul and higher-self connection with God.

The *Emerald Tablet* speaks to the philosophy of the entire world. The three energies that influence all things are the masculine energies projecting force/intention, the feminine energies determining form/support in expression, and the spirit energies of inspiration/fire.

Spirit permeates all issues and all matter, dense and dross.

Spiritual Light can be compared to the electricity in our house. They are both invisible to the physical eyes, yet we can tell their presence by seeing how they affect us. Electricity turns on the lights when we turn on the light switch.

We can tell when Spirit is working in our lives. We can see miracles taking place. We can see and feel blessings lifting our life, bringing greater continuity and grace. Synchronicities are common. We can become aware and check in on how our flow is working in our life, whether we are in grace and in balance or if we have emotional baggage to address.

We can see the effect of Higher Light through the ultimate mirror—that of blessings, miracles, and grace flowing through our lives.

The concept of mirrors is effective for our personal lives, and shows us the kind of energies that are working within us and through people with whom we are in close contact. We might not see things working in our lives and may often wonder what is going on. At the same time, we might see others around us with dysfunctional lives going on and see a mirror of what and how we are creating in our own lives.

If our phone goes out, it may be a mirror back to us, that we need to pay attention to spiritual matters in our life while the phone is being fixed. It may be that our lives would be well-served to pay more attention to relationships or family.

On a larger scale, the world has seen a pandemic on a global scale. The world might be wondering, "What is going on? How did this happen?" If we meditate on the situation, we might see a world of people, and many countries, that are not treating each other with Love. Wars are being fought all over the world. In the midst of hate everywhere, humanity Is being forced to band together to find solutions, though social interaction is being limited, especially in groups. Curfews are being imposed. By necessity, humanity is recognizing through this mirror that their world based on judgment and blame needs to change.

If we look for higher meaning in all things, we can see a higher purpose, most of the time, for things happening in the world or in our lives. It is up to each of us to pay attention and pray.

"When we choose to be aligned, we attract people that are a blessing and enable us to move gracefully through our soul lessons."

- John Pollock

CHAPTER VIII — RELATIONSHIPS & ENERGY

Relationships are a very complex area for everyone, and sometimes confusing and difficult to understand. Romantic relationships involve attracting a partner with similar energies, yet bringing issues that each partner can learn from and that each partner can contribute to in the physical world, as well as on spiritual levels. Most romantic relationships seem to involve a karmic bond that keeps drawing the partners together through rocky times.

We are often attracted to a person who is like another person from the past who disappointed us. The challenge is to have another opportunity to grow in understanding ourselves, to stay balanced, and to proceed with grace to make a relationship work.

Chemistry, excitement, and sexual attraction seem to be based on a combination of attraction to the physical package and like-experience with common issues to be processed together and individually. People energetically feel drawn to others who have something in common with them. This energy is called "magnetism"—the more commonalities, the stronger the magnetism.

Lasting relationships tend to have good reasons for both parties to stay together. Chemistry brings people together, but for a relationship to last, it has to evolve toward the purpose of the Holy Spirit.

Successful business and networking relationships are based upon members being mutually beneficial to each other and operating together for a positive purpose. It is always a good idea to ask in prayer, and program our life to have the right people in our lives. Our innermost desires connect energetically to attract our best reality.

Our auric field will always attract a reality that mirrors lessons and the blessings from our level of growth. A positive, caring, and compassionate disposition attracts a positive influence and blessings from higher levels of Light, raising our consciousness and benefiting our life. Our belief systems and judgments inherently project a consistent intention that supports our own creation. Our mirrors are for our personal use to see our own progress, and to see the consequences of the energies we are emitting.

It is sometimes hard to realize that there are energetic connections with all situations, especially with relationships that are challenging for us. On the surface, it looks like a relationship is for the purpose of selling real estate or hiring good people to work for a company to make a profit, etc. The need to earn financial support is a driving necessity for ourselves and for our families. Providing a service is something we learn along the way, and with experience, we bring income for ourselves and our family.

If we look past the immediate requirements of every situation, we find that working out mutual benefit for all concerned is what is required to resolve conflicts that arises. The spiritual lessons are to experience maintaining balance with ourselves and Spirit while, at the same time, experiencing a win-win outcome for everyone.

Personal relationships require harmony with the Holy Spirit and living in grace. Every situation seems to be different, but the long-term solution always involves infusing more Light and raising the difficult situations and our relationship to a higher level of consciousness.

Albert Einstein once said that the answer to a problem is never found at the same level of consciousness in which it was created.

Having a sexual union on the physical plane is a complicated affair. It involves sexual attraction in the physical, as well as attraction between the energy fields of the partners in relationship. A romantic relationship may be long-term or temporary, depending on compatibility and whether the karmic lessons that are complimentary have been resolved. When relationships end, many times one partner is complete with the process while unresolved issues go with the other partner to be addressed in the next relationship they enter into.

Programming our lives serves us well on many levels. On a mundane level, when we are overwhelmed with too many people or clients, or too many family issues to handle, we can pray that we have enough time and resources to handle the confusion. Magically, the communications even out and we are blessed with solutions.

In higher dimensions, we are aware of our Philosopher's Stone in prayer, and manifesting our soul's purpose. We ask for grace and guidance. We are attracting the where-with-all to manifest what we need and want to accomplish our vision.

The workings of Spirit play a big part behind the scenes. Our energy field automatically attracts our heart's desire. Our best choice is to align with the infusion of Light and prayers in our life. When we choose to be aligned, we attract people that are a blessing and enable us to move gracefully through our soul lessons. We experience more love, joy, and success on our path.

"When we are working with Higher Beings of Light,
we ask for Highest guidance and wisdom,
as well as insight on our path."

- John Pollock

CHAPTER IX - ENERGY, CONSCIOUSNESS & AWARENESS

We enter the living room and the phone rings. Immediately, a friend or family member pops into our mind. Or perhaps it works the other way around—we enter the living room and a friend or family member pops into our mind, and then the phone rings. Either way, when we answer the phone, we are half-surprised to hear that very person's voice!

Likewise, a family member or a close friend may come into our mind, so we call them to find out if they need help or if anything is wrong. We are half-surprised again to discover that *they* were just thinking of *us,* and perhaps were even in dire straits and needed our help. We realize that we have intuitively sensed their anxiety and fear, and the sense of importance to call right away.

It is well-documented that twins often have this close connection with each other. They can often tell if traumatic events are being experienced by the other twin.

People often ponder and dismiss such occurrences as unexplainable coincidence, and then go on their way. One time, I received a call from a good friend who had a very strong feeling that her son was in danger. She was also intuitive and, together, we took that information quite seriously. We prayed together getting centered, grounded, and aligned with Christ Holy Spirit, as well as the Angels. We prayed for her son to be surrounded in Light and to be protected from harm. We later found out that her son was aboard a bus traveling in the mountains west of Denver, and at that moment, he made a decision to change his travel plans and get off the bus. The bus went on to have a catastrophic accident further down the road. Literally, by the Grace of God, he was saved.

It is common for family members to be awakened during the night at the exact time that a loved one passes away and crosses over to the other side. Later they might have visions and dreams where a loved one has come to them. They might also feel the strong energy of their loved one indicating that they are still loved from the other side.

How are these events to be explained?

Although these and many more events may appear to be unexplainable in our three-dimensional world, they allude to an influence from Spirit in other dimensions. The presence of God can be seen working through all life. God energetically contributes a positive influence of grace and inspiration behind the scenes.

The simple answer to our question is "intention." The spark of Light within empowers humanity with the ability to energetically create our reality in the physical world. This ability to create extends into the universe and all creation, and comes with the sharing of Light from God in the original creation of humankind. We were created with free will and empowerment through Light. The more we choose to align with the Love and Light of God's original purpose, the more we can open to receive the support, nurturing, and success that is meant for us to experience.

Grace and enlightenment are gifts from God as we travel the road of fulfillment, joy, and illumination amidst a world filled with illusion.

Passion, desire, and inspiration put force into our intention. This seems to happen automatically, without our having to think about it. Manifesting what we want happens in a split second with an impulse and spontaneous creativity. A clear focus is helpful in providing a sharp picture and quick action from the universe.

A good example of this process is to set our intention of what we want to experience or where we want to dream-travel before going to bed at night. At first, we might think that our dreams are not real. Actually, our dreams may span a multitude of dimensions helping to lift up our life-experience. Affirming what positive reality we want in the physical also has a tendency to bring loving life-experience, fulfillment, and positive adventure through grace.

The entire manifesting process is more far-reaching than we might first suspect. Every time we think of another person or an energy in Spirit, we reach out in our soul-essence to create a new etheric road or energetic pathway connecting with them. This line, or energetic pathway, carries both a charge and a flow of wisdom, understanding, consciousness, and vitality in the physical. What is transferred is again dependent upon intention.

Our intention determines whether we are requesting guidance and blessings from Spirit, or whether we are sending prayers and support to another by being a conduit and aligning with Spirit.

Meditation is a process of prayer:

We first call ourselves into alignment with the energy flows within the body. Then we call our truth forward from within our heart into perfect alignment with our Soul and Higher Self, Divine Father and Mother God, and the Purest heart of Love and Light of all creation, the All That Is.

We call ourselves to ground with Mother Earth for energies of nurturing and support, balance of Spirit with the physical, and empowerment in the physical through alignment with Light.

This brings us into an altered state where we connect with Spirit and lose track of time and orientation. We sit in meditation, channeling peace, Love, and Light. This raises our vibration. From there, we can ask in prayer for our worldly needs to be met, and give thanks for the miracles coming to us. Meditation clears out fear and anxiety, helping us appreciate our blessings.

This is a good place from which to work. We can ask Christ Holy Spirit for healing for ourselves and others. We ask to connect with others with the intention of balance in giving and receiving, and open to input from Spirit. We hold a space for Light to flow through us for everyone's Highest good. When we are working with Higher Beings of Light, we ask for Highest guidance and wisdom, as well as insight on our path.

To connect with other Sacred Energies, as well as with other people, we put forth our request to the Light to help make the connection and proceed in the Highest service and the Highest expression for ourselves.

The Angels tell us that we would do well to infuse Light, peace, humor, and grace into our earthly expression and experience. We have unlimited potential to create a more joyful and fulfilling life while enjoying and learning from those experiences we attract at soul level. We pray to infuse greater Light into our lives. We are blessed!

"Spirituality as our philosophy of living
has brought ancient truths back around to create
an increasing awareness and a positive environment
to elevate the consciousness of humanity."

- John Pollock

CHAPTER X — FOCUS FOR STABILITY

We already know that Light follows our intention. Before philosophy and science came into vogue, motivational speaking and sales were coming together to give us a way to create a more positive and lucrative lifestyle for ourselves. Changing our lifestyle to include everyone in a win-win philosophy brings success for all. We must all ascend together to make meaningful and lasting change.

Spirituality as our philosophy of living has brought ancient truths back around to create an increasing awareness and a positive environment to elevate the consciousness of humanity.

Most political and economic structures in the world today are based on the mass belief that resources and opportunities are limited. It seems that we see confirmation everywhere we look. Fear of not getting enough or fear of not getting our share, keeps us striving for more. "What we see is what we get." It's funny that our mass belief in lack, or that we are victims, is where we seem to be getting confirmation these days.

What Spirit has continually shown us through history is that when times are bleak, creativity and new innovation saves the day. That is what America is known for. It is interesting that our founding fathers printed "In God We Trust" on our currency. It serves us well to keep reminding ourselves that our country is founded in God. We want to keep this awareness to keep this gift operating in our reality.

Whenever we start believing in get-rich schemes, our political-economic system and governments take a hit. Whether we can see through a promotion or not, the old adage still rings loud and clear, "If it looks too good to be true, it probably is." Only a system that requires everyone to do their part builds a strong foundation.

This brings us back to our spiritual approach to life that permeates all areas of honesty with our self, honesty with others, and integrity in all our affairs.

Many years ago, a movie called *The Flim Flam Man* was produced with George C. Scott. The main character would scam people in elaborate plots, promising exorbitant returns on their investments. He justified his shenanigans by saying that you can't take advantage of an honest man. The honest man wouldn't try to trick people out of their funds, so he wouldn't get involved in the first place. Trying to take advantage of others in a financial venture is what sets us up to be taken advantage of ourselves. What goes around comes around.

In the area of personal integrity, there was a book written called *Codependent No More: How to Stop Controlling Others and Start Caring for Yourself* by Melody Beattie. The basic message was to stop asking someone else to do something if you can do it for yourself. We re-train ourselves to discontinue dysfunctional behavior and be successful in all areas of our life.

Everyone uses something to get what they want out of life. In an energetic universe, we release life-circumstances to Spirit for answers to our prayers. Essentially, what we are doing is asking a Loving God to bring Light to bear on circumstances and situations in order to bring about manifesting in our life. We plant seeds of desire and receive blessings and miracles. Remember, we are asking for blessings for circumstances, not control over other people. With prayer, people will usually change very dramatically as a result of blessings of Light for all those concerned. Situations bring a surprise change and a positive slant.

Years ago, while unfolding on my path of service, I learned a valuable lesson about working with energy. I was visiting at a restaurant with a very gifted friend. She picked up intuitively that someone in the restaurant had a certain difficulty going on in her life. I was then looking around the room to see if I could sense who it was. I asked what she was "seeing" in her mind's eye.

She said she could not tell who we were picking up on, but she could see that my soul-essence was going out from my Third-Eye chakra and was traveling around the room searching for the person that she had described. My intention to locate the person in question was sending out a stream of Light. We ask and receive Light from Spirit, and with our intention, we send Light to do our bidding—all in line with spiritual purpose.

This brings us to the process of aligning energetically with different levels of Light. When we call ourselves into alignment with our truth within our heart, we are starting to focus on the spark of Light that is within, that spark of

God that is within every person. We can ask Spirit to help us feel in our Heart chakra the Light welling up, vibrating, and expanding around our body. This is the highest aspect of our soul-essence that is a part of God, which we may come to know as part of our physical embodiment. We may need to call Spirit to come forward through the essence of our truth to become aware of what this part of our God-essence feels like.

When we call ourselves to ground, we are connecting with the feminine energies that are an aspect of God and a gift to humanity in supporting our physical life on this planet. Not only does Mother Earth support our physical well-being, she also supports us energetically.

The feminine Light from Mother Earth flows nurturing through us and to us and our families—in our political, sociological, economic, and all aspects of form that God is to take expression. All forms of management and efficiency take place through our feminine aspect of God. When we connect to Mother Earth, we focus on our awareness of her great love for humanity and tremendous energy vibrating from her. We feel this energy rising up our feet and legs, into our body, and supporting us in our personal expression. We feel the vibration and expansion of energy up our legs, expanding our Base chakra in empowerment and permeating our body.

When we call forward our Soul and Higher Self, we are extending our expression upward. Our Soul is the energy body that is our auric field and attracts lessons in the physical that extend into our spiritual essence above. Our Higher Self is the highest expression of our self as an individual, and energetic extension of soul, which is both "at one" with our soul's purpose and, at the same time, the pure expression of God. When we call forward Soul and Higher Self, we are accessing higher levels of energy and Light to reach higher vibration streaming down into the Third-Eye and Crown chakras of the head, and tapping a sense of higher consciousness, wisdom, and understanding above.

It is good to know that the chakras tend to open in a spiral *outward* from the body. The Third-Eye chakra opens *inward* to tap a multitude of dimensions, reaching visions, moving through time, and traveling to other levels of creation. The Third-Eye chakra works with the Crown chakra to bring Light into our being in expression of our soul truth and infusing Higher Light and guidance into our path.

For a six-year period in Denver, Colorado, Rheana Jackson and I teamed up to facilitate a Healing and Manifesting meetup group. The group would meet in coffee shops or restaurants in the Denver Metro area.

Our agenda was to meet, invoke Spirit, and share experiences where Christ Holy Spirit would work to bring Light and miracles into our lives, and to put forth prayers to assist everyone. The prayer invocation would always begin with a process to center, ground, and align personal energies with energies of the group for highest and best use. We met every week with the members who were drawn together that particular week. There were several hundred members who all participated at one time or another.

At one point, after many years, I asked Rheana what she got from the meeting group. Her response was that it had brought stability into her life.

Of course, there was support for the members and the miracles that would happen from time to time. One member was unemployed. He met a new wife within several months and relocated with a new job to Hawaii. Stories like this one were commonplace and always celebrated with Spirit.

The one thing that was always emphasized was our prayer to center, ground, and align through the Violet Light of transformation. In visiting with other members, it was clear that they were releasing emotional baggage from the past and empowering a higher purpose in addition to experiencing more joy and grace in their lives.

I have gone into depth in my first two books, presenting the process to center, ground, and align with Spirit. The importance is to bring in energies with which we are familiar, that are compatible with each other and operating within us to present a solid front to hold Light for growth and expression.

It is about expansion of Light within and assisting our growth process, uplifting our spiritual essence. Frequent meditation and prayer serve to help us to raise our vibration rate, allowing us to connect more easily with Spirit. Without centering, grounding, and aligning, there are gaps in the levels of Light, allowing invasion by other energies, and throwing us out of balance.

Centering, grounding, and aligning with Spirit holds Light on all dimensions and levels leading to Source level, the Mind of God. It allows us to carry more Light, achieve balance between Spirit and the physical, as well as between masculine and feminine energies of the physical world and dimensions above and beyond. By consistent meditation and a focus on aligning with the Light, we strengthen our connection with Source God and our expression of Light.

"It is up to each of us to choose the spiritual energies that we are drawn to and want to experience next."

- John Pollock

CHAPTER XI — EXPRESSION OF LIGHT & SELF-MASTERY

With all the dissension between different cultural, religious, and political beliefs, we still find a common thread of truth that is Light shining through to humanity, assisting in the evolution of humankind. Even through the darkest times in history, the Light works through everyone possible, and to the greatest extent possible, to bring wisdom, understanding, and higher guidance into our lives. Prayer and meditation take many forms, including song and dance, with Light always flowing through to us and uplifting us.

In a lifetime, we are exposed to different religious thought and different cultures, all making a contribution to us. It is up to each of us to choose the spiritual energies that we are drawn to and want to experience next.

We meditate to bring in more Light. We set our intention to focus in on our life, our resources, and the projects that we want to accomplish. We call ourselves to center, ground, and align ourselves with Spirit on all levels. We meditate to clear, receive guidance, and charge our energy field for right action empowerment. Our energy field has Light working through it. We become aware of the movement of Light.

We ask for highest wisdom and understanding, and then listen on many levels of intuition to receive guidance, feedback, peace, and fulfillment from Spirit. After setting forth our intention and desires in prayer, circumstances have a tendency to fall into place. We go forward in a state of grace and remain flexible and open to receive.

From our center and alignment with Spirit, we feel our energetic connection with God. The Light is welling up inside and expanding outward around our body. The Light that we have been calling in is higher consciousness that has a consistency that we can feel. It has a buoyancy to it. We feel a subtle electric current vibrating our body. Light comes from Source God and descends through the different levels and through bringers of Light to humanity to answer prayers and to bless humankind.

Johrei and Reiki healing are two Japanese modes of healing that use symbols, Christ energies, and prayer altar. The technique for sending distance healing is to pray to bring in Light and charge our own energy field, and then visualize the person who needs the healing. The higher vibration and electromagnetic charge in our auric field then automatically transfer to that person. This is an example of how energy lines are established and connections are made in the physical world. Our desire to bless someone and our intention to help create healing, establish energy lines behind the scenes to continue working. We want to be aware and be sure to send *positive* thoughts to others, because our thoughts continue to have an effect on people and situations, much like prayer.

Light comes through different avenues. Many different situations call for different techniques in connecting for clearing and balance, for guidance, and connecting for healing.

"We develop a closer bond with Spirit as we begin to realize the vast storehouse of unlimited Love that is our heritage and birthright."

- John Pollock

Chapter XII — Hermes Trismegistus & Alchemy

Hermes Thrice-Great Trismegistus spoke of meditating to use a process known as "alchemy" to flash-burn issues of karma, both individual and those shared with humanity. Alchemy is used to assist us to release emotional and mental issues that would otherwise weigh down our spiritual essence, thus bringing illumination and uplifting our energetic-spiritual growth. The process of alchemy to transform our Light essence has evolved from the information given to us in the *Emerald Tablet* teaching from Hermes Thrice-Great Trismegistus, over ten thousand years ago. The Light working through the

Emerald Tablet is a clear but deep Emerald Green color for truth in manifesting and creating our spiritual truth on Earth. Otherwise, the Light coming through Hermes would be a bright crystal-clear color for clearing, teaching, and assisting to lift up our spiritual essence.

Hermes worked to help us understand the changing consciousness on the Earth plane and align our soul consciousness with Spirit. I have gone into great depth in *Prayers for All Occasions*, and *MYSTIC* regarding understanding and use of this higher knowledge.

Once we align through soul, the next process involves traveling through our spiritual imagination up to the Mind of God, the source of All That Is, to bring Light energies down to be a part of the ONE THING. The ONE THING, according to Hermes, is the height of God that we in humanity pray to through the various religions, cultures, and the lines of historical significance. When we connect with Mind in prayer and bring the fire essence down to combine with the ONE THING, the miracles happen for humanity on Earth. Our most sincere prayers are answered.

Just as the Hathors teach that we must each take responsibility for our own growth and make changes in ourselves, so too, does Hermes talk of this through his teachings of the Philosopher's Stone.

The ancient teachings of the Hermetic Philosophy were taught in the Gnostic Gospels by Hermes Thrice-Great Trismegistus. The teachings were not a religion, but rather, spiritual teachings involving the energetic structure of the universe, the raising of consciousness, and enlightenment of humankind to transcend the physical plane. The teachings are to be used with whatever religious discoveries the seeker of truth is led to on his or her path of enlightenment.

All creation is made up of Love and Light. That is who God is, and that is what God has to work with in His creation of life.

Everything that is alive has a soul. The soul was created by God to nurture life on Earth and to sustain the many lower levels of life within. The Light is under pressure to infuse Light into all creation and to return on high, swirling within all dimensions. One of the most basic understandings of life is that all creation is formulated with different levels, having different functions and varying levels of consciousness.

A biological understanding of the human body brings energetic communication between cells, as well as with the environment. The world maintains consciousness at the elemental levels, helping to sustain life for the plant and animal kingdoms, as well as for humankind. The Angels tell us that the interconnected chakra system enables us to understand the energetic structure and consciousness of our existence on Earth. The rising chakras and the division of labor are a good way to understand the structure of the universe. The different Angels and Beings of Light are at different levels of consciousness and have differing purposes in service to God. Archangels Raphael, Michael, Gabriel, and Uriel are known to be in service to humankind.

As we are growing up, most of the focus of humanity revolves around relieving discomfort and solving the problems arising in the physical world. However, as we gain maturity, we appreciate more and more, the blessings of Spirit and the beautiful energies of Grace that is shared with our spiritual essence. We develop a closer bond with Spirit as we begin to realize the vast storehouse of unlimited Love that is our heritage and birthright. It is to be reborn again in higher consciousness and merge our soul essence with the eternal Light of God.

Alchemy

In ancient days, alchemy was known as a science to use spiritual energy to change the chemical make-up of lead to create gold. The purpose has evolved in psychological and spiritual circles to now refer to the higher gold of Spirit to reach man's transformation and his enlightenment.

There was an old alchemist saying: "Aurum Nostrum Non-Est Aurum Vulgi: Our gold is not common gold."

The energetic stages of alchemy are as follows:

STEP 1 - CALCINATION

$\mathcal{M}$editation is used to ignite a process known as "alchemy" to flash-burn issues of karma. Alchemy is all about transformation. We are freeing our spirit-essence from ego and self-doubts, fears, core beliefs, self-deception, pride, and arrogance. Emotional issues, harsh judgments, and our soul are flash-burned and reduced to ashes. Alchemy is used to assist us to release emotional and mental issues that would otherwise weigh down our spiritual essence. We are purified in the transformational fire of the Holy Spirit.

STEP 2 - DISSOLUTION

Our false sense of self is brought to the surface. We become aware of traumatizing memories and how they might be affecting our self and others. We are shocked and begin a process of spiritual awakening. We become aware of our denial, resistance, and avoidance patterns.

STEP 3 - SEPARATION

We differentiate between thoughts and feelings, not blaming or excusing behavior but experiencing our feelings and thoughts side by side to discover our authentic self. At this stage we see and take responsibility for our own thoughts and feelings.

STEP 4 - CONJUNCTION

Unconscious beliefs, thoughts, and feelings bubble to the surface. Journaling and introspection help us to see and accept our authentic self. We identify the parts we want to keep and those we wish to integrate into our expression.

STEP 5 - FERMENTATION

The conscious and unconscious levels of mind are allowing the putrification and decomposition of our former selves that no longer serve our spiritual transformation. This stage might be called "the dark night of the soul." This process involves inner process work, stillness, and insight.

STEP 6 - DISTILLATION

There is further purification and integration of spiritual realizations that have come to us. This stage is referred to as self-realization or enlightenment. This is a time of living with inner peace and living in the present moment. When we let go of the past and future journey expectations during this process, we experience profound inner transformation and expanding awareness.

STEP 7 - COAGULATION

*I*n this stage, we have broken free of the influence of lower mind. The patterns of the past are released to Spirit. We are living with the flow of Spirit moving through our soul, and synchronicities in our life are commonplace.

Hermes refers to this alignment of our soul consciousness on the Earth plane and soul energies moving up through the dimensions as aligning on a spiritual axis. This is a vertical alignment through the higher and higher levels to Mind, Source God. This is the infusion of Light spoken of in the establishment of the medicine wheel vortex energies. Hermes was speaking from inspiration given to him directly by Mind, Source God HImself. It is a gift to humanity for teaching and assisting to lift up all humankind.

It is important that spiritual alchemy is known and taught in the ancient *Emerald Tablet* of Hermes. It is a precursor to subsequent spiritual disciplines presenting their own unique way for the transformation of humanity and creating a shift in consciousness. The Angels say that we have a long life to live, that we might as well pray to the Angels for grace, joy, and fulfillment along the way. Hermes was concerned for humankind that we were many times caught up in the drama and challenges of the three-dimensional world and losing sight, not giving enough importance to our path of evolution. In addition to experiencing and expressing Love, we are all here for the spiritual purpose of raising our consciousness and returning to our essence in Light.

The Gnostic Gospels provide a tremendous work of spiritual knowledge to help lift us up in consciousness, and to demonstrate enlightenment through our expression of the Light. The potential for growth and expansion of consciousness is unlimited, as are the different paths to transformation. Each person's own path of self-discovery and pursuing the spiritual study to which we are drawn. We are all on Earth to follow our hearts, to raise our vibrations, to lift up our awareness, and to follow our inspiration with guidance.

"Know thyself. Love thyself. Nurture thyself!"

- John Pollock

CHAPTER XIII —EMPOWERMENT & NOURISHMENT

The Goddess Hathor was revered and her image was carved on most other gods' temples in Egypt. Her reign followed that of the crocodile God known as Sobek who represented strength during his reign. When Goddess Hathor's reign began, she incorporated the strength of her predecessor and brought forward strength and clarity aligning with the All That Is, Source God, also referred to as the Mind of God. Her reign ended with the Egyptian Goddess Isis who took Hathor's place of leadership in history. Goddess Hathor was worshipped for thousands of years starting in 4000 BCE and lasting until 500 AD, with

Isis gradually taking predominance in 1550-1070 BCE in myth, having resurrected her slain husband Osiris. To put this into perspective, the Egyptian pharaoh Amenhotep IV, who later changed his name to Akhenaten, had a seventeen-year reign from 1351-1334 BCE, changing the worship of the many Gods to the worship of the One God perceived as the Source "**ONE MIND**" flowing into the ONE THING. They worshipped the ONE THING, which was called the Sun God or "The Disk."

We spoke of Goddess Hathor in Chapter Two when we spoke of the ascension of a civilization and the strength of integrity, focus, and empowerment that she held with her many followers to accomplish such a tremendous feat together.

Goddess Hathor holds a solid connection to ground and, acting as a strong root system, holds a firm connection to Mother Earth while the upper limbs may be swaying with the wind. She anchors energies in the Universe in much the same way. Her energies are opaque and appear like milk with a thick and creamy texture with minerals to nourish life on the physical plane and a complete set of energies for balance to nourish all levels of life in the cosmos. Her Light is strength and gentleness, bringing a fullness and richness to life. Nourishment of our spiritual essence is what grows the Light within and uplifts us on our journey of ascension.

Zeus was known as the Father of the Gods. His feminine counterpart was Hera who would assist in completion of karma and would celebrate when karma was satisfied and issues were released. Goddess Hathor was closely aligned with Hera and served in the gentle nurturing of humanity, but also, in the holding of Sacred Space and protection for the powerful Sun God Ra, also known as "The Disk." Hathor embodied the feminine aspect of God—nurturing, support, and the principle of nourishing life in all dimensions. She brought complete and balanced energies to humankind with such Love and nourishment.

We work with Goddess Hathor feminine energy in balance with the masculine willpower and goal-oriented prayers. We put forth our desires to work with Spirit to manifest our spiritual path with guidance. We plant seeds of our visions in prayer while holding Sacred energies to fruition. We also remain open to guidance and creative input to advance us on our spiritual path.

Opening to the feminine side of our energy field is the way we access Spirit.

Our balanced expression is about honoring our truth inside and honoring others as well. Our intention in prayer is to manifest a win-win for everyone. It is about opening our hearts and our feminine side—"feeling" energies— allowing our prayers and spirit blessings to flow through our lives. We trust Spirit to move our situations and reality into Divine flow and bring nurturing into our lives.

In meditation, we energetically use a deep tone like a fog horn, and instruments like the Australian didgeridoo, to clear lower chakras. We chant with the "OM" symbol to balance our energy field and connect with Spirit. We use the Tibetan Bells with a sharp piercing sound to connect with our higher chakras and higher spirit vibrations infusing Light.

In our everyday lives, we express ourselves for support in positive endeavors that connect us with nature and open our energy field to prayers working to enhance our spiritual purpose and earthly expression. Our self-appreciation then becomes manifest in our physical reality.

Know thyself. Love thyself. Nurture thyself!

"The high energies of compassion and enlightenment
consume clouds of lower consciousness
of the worldly plane."

- John Pollock

Chapter XIV — Buddha Consciousness

To Buddhists, Krishna is known as God. There are many avatars that tell us they are a doorway to Krishna consciousness. Rama is one such avatar, another is Buddha, and there are as many as one hundred others. But there is only one being of Light that says that He is the embodiment of God himself, and that is Krishna.

God has given humankind free will. We all have the right to focus our consciousness in the physical world, or be lifted into higher consciousness through prayer and meditation. Wisdom from Spirit guides our growth and choices on our life path.

Buddhism is about meditation. Buddhist meditation is about being still at times, and also incorporates rhythmic graceful movement with the energies of the bell, the gong, the clapper, drums, and sounding boards. The meditations are about being mindful with God.

Life is seen as preparation for the hereafter, and then preparation again for incarnation. Life is a cycle. Buddha teaches of the wheel of karma, that each person must experience every station along the karmic wheel of life.

When we see Buddha, we feel and relate to the energies of Buddha consciousness which are all around us in nature and humanity. We connect to the One Buddha Mind.

Meditation is for enlightenment, spiritual awakening, and inner peace. Physical and emotional healing comes with integration of enlightenment, including the Japanese healing disciplines of Reiki and Johrei.

The high energies of compassion and enlightenment consume clouds of lower consciousness of the worldly plane and lift up the vibration rates in meditation using the well-known mantras and healing with Johrei and Reiki. Even though the development of these two healing disciplines originated sixty miles apart on the same island, both Johrei and Reiki use the same powerful symbol DAI-KO-MYO (pronounced di-ko-me-oh) as the basis for both disciplines.

When asked what Buddhism is all about, the answer is *compassion*. The celestial embodiment of compassion and enlightenment is Avalokiteshvara who wrote perhaps the best-known Buddhist mantra "Om Mani Padme Hum." Another name for Avalokiteshvara is Chenrezig. In Tibet, Chenrezig is known as the Buddha of Love and Compassion.

Kalu Rinpoche discussed the meaning of the six syllables of the mantra "Om Mani Padme Hum." It encompasses all of the Buddhist teachings.

Om Mani Padme Hum

OM blesses us and helps us to achieve perfection in the practice of generosity.

MA blesses us and helps us to perfect the practice of pure ethics.

NI blesses us and helps us to achieve perfection in the practice of tolerance and patience.

PAD blesses us and helps us to achieve the perfection of perseverance.

ME blesses us and helps us to achieve perfection in the practice of concentration.

HUM blesses us and helps us to achieve perfection in the practice of wisdom.

Kalu Rinpoche said, "What could be more meaningful than to say the mantra and accomplish the six perfections?"

The mantra helps us to raise our vibration in awareness, seeking perfection in six different areas.

Mantras assist us in raising our spiritual awareness in everyday living, and the use of Reiki and Johrei energies consume clouds of lower consciousness in purification, charging our energy field with Light. Chanting brings more Light.

We are told that when we see a picture or a statue of Buddha, we can expand. We can feel and sense and relate to the energies of Buddha consciousness all around us in nature and humanity. We connect to the One Buddha Mind.

Ayurvedic knowledge helps to minimize the four pains that every entity must suffer by incarnation in the physical. These are the birth process, aging, illness, and experiencing death. The transcendental approach to enlightenment is to merge with the Supreme Krishna consciousness. The process continues in the life eternal— after life in the physical, in our ascension into life everlasting.

The Buddhist teaching says that the spirit of compassion and enlightenment is the true nature of humankind and resides within the Heart chakra, and is linked to God. It is for us to expand this connection and be charged, blessed, and lifted in awareness. The confusion of the speech aspect of our Being is transformed into enlightened awareness.

It is interesting to note that the Buddhist energies are very difficult to distinguish from Christ Holy Spirit in the etheric. They are both a fine sparkling Gold color and are experienced at a high vibration.

"We need to prepare our physical bodies and mindset for such intense transformation and processing by caring for our health and well-being."

- John Pollock

CHAPTER XV — QABALAH & INITIATION

The Qabalah TREE OF LIFE was ancient wisdom given to the Hebrews for the benefit of all humankind. The Hebrews have said that the TREE OF LIFE is a diagram, a glyph that is based upon symbols and their relationship to ourselves, to other symbols, and their relationship to Source God. The TREE OF LIFE is a dynamic multidimensional whirling of energies that is said to be a projection of the Mind of God. We see the same relationships in spirit dimensions and physical dimensions as we see in the glyph of the TREE OF LIFE. We may be surprised to find out that they are energetically one and the same.

The levels of the TREE OF LIFE correspond to the levels of Spirit and the movement of Light as it descends from Source God through all the sephirot in succession, then reaching its destination in the story of creation on Earth for humanity.

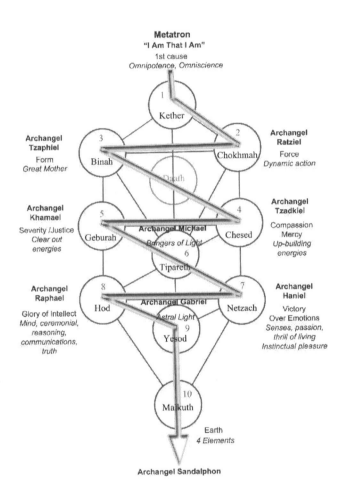

The teaching about the TREE OF LIFE could not be taught in the third dimension, rather it is knowledge founded in higher dimensions of Spirit accessed above the level of written study and rational thought. Higher knowledge is accessed through meditation and sincere pursuit of truth. Higher wisdom is tapped during meditation with symbols stimulating higher creativity, and communicating through visions and intuitive understanding that must be experienced to appreciate. Archangels and other beings of Light teach us by blending their energies with our energy field, thereby blessing us to raise our vibration rate and experience a higher form of expressing ourselves.

Learning is received through higher levels of our spiritual essence and through connection with higher Light and enlightened guidance. The TREE OF LIFE is all about one initiation after another.

Initiation may be described here as the receiving of an instantaneous burst of subtle Light energy to our personal energy field, bringing an expansion of consciousness and an acceleration of spiritual growth. It brings an opening to new awareness and a permanent change.

Initiation leads to additional initiation and yet higher consciousness, leading to a process of higher and higher transformation. No matter how far we progress on our path of enlightenment, there is always more to go. The potential in spiritual growth is always unlimited, just as God is unlimited in His expression.

The sephirot contain energies for initiation, and archetypes symbolizing the spiritual teaching associated with ten different Hebrew names of God.

At the top of the glyph is *Ain Soph Aur* which means *Nothingness, Limitless, Light*. This is the bright Gold and White Light of God that extends into the TREE OF LIFE and descends downward to humankind. "The roots of the TREE OF LIFE are in heaven." The sephirot that follow have Metatron and Archangels holding the energies for teaching the Archetypes and for initiation.

Metatron is an aspect of God, and is the representative of "Kether." Metatron has been instrumental in Creation on a molecular level and brings energies for transformation to humankind. His energies oversee the process of bringing Light, involution of Light into the physical, and evolution of Light working within humanity to raise all humankind back to Source God. "Kether" is the first sephira upon the descent of Light, the archetype being First Cause. From a greater point of understanding, this is the first spark of conception of whatever is to be created—*the first thought*.

The understanding and progression of Light in the TREE OF LIFE has been presented in some detail in my first two books; however, there are several points to be made to add perspective to our previous discussion.

The TREE OF LIFE gives us teaching about the nature of the sephirot and how they give us different levels of understanding about ourselves. At the same time, the TREE OF LIFE teaches us about multiple levels of Spirit and growth in consciousness on our spiritual path. Light is teaching us that we are a part of The TREE OF LIFE *symbolically,* and part of the TREE OF LIFE *literally* in the flesh.

Light descends in the Lightning bolt pattern to the right column to "Chokhmah," represented by Archangel Ratziel, Divine Father, with Archetype of Force, and then on to the left column to "Binah," represented by Archangel Tzaphiel, Divine Mother, with Archetype of Form. When working with a sephira in the right column called "Mercy," which is masculine, be sure to also work with corresponding sephira on the left column called "Severity," which is feminine. This maintains balanced masculine and feminine energies within the center pillar called "Mildness." It's about balance in prayer and balance in meditation. This applies not only to Force and Form, but also to Mercy and Severity-Justice, and to Victory over emotions and Glory Ceremonial of Mind.

The energies of the TREE OF LIFE are strong and must be kept in balance. When I was first introduced to the TREE OF LIFE, I met a man who had gotten in over his head and would never forget the aggravation of imbalanced meditation.

In addition to balance of male and female within meditations on the TREE OF LIFE, we also have to consider balance in the four dimensions (or four worlds) for creating. The Qabalah Cross brings integration on all levels in all dimensions, with a separate but connected TREE OF LIFE on each level of Emanation, Creation, Formation, and Action.

The Four Worlds

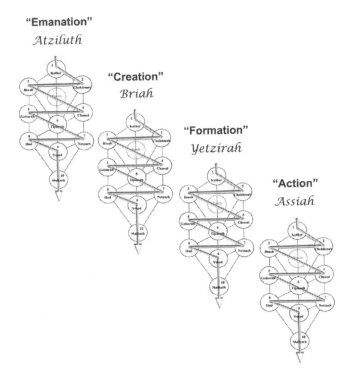

"Emanation"
Atziluth

"Creation"
Briah

"Formation"
Yetzirah

"Action"
Assiah

If we take a broad view, we see the TREE OF LIFE as a symbolic representation of initiations and energetic pathways descending down from the *Ain Soph Aur: Nothing, Limitless, Light* at Source. The Light travels down into all levels and dimensions, infusing Light into all creation.

If we take the short and narrow view, we can imagine the outline of a human body, head and shoulders in the physical plane, overlaying the sephirot of the TREE OF LIFE. Energies start at the Ain Soph Aur and drop down through our Crown chakra following the pattern of the Lightning Bolt.

When we are off-balance, it is often hard to get in touch with our own issues. We invoke powerful energies of Spirit to blend with ourselves, charging our energy field for expansion of consciousness and healing.

This one meditation brings strong spiritual healing into all levels and all dimensions to dissolve issues of thought and emotions to empower balance in our lives. Know that time and space will be needed to process the Shifts this initiation makes in our lives.

Meditation of the Qabalah Cross

Information is given in detail in *Prayers for All Occasions* and *MYSTIC*. Frequent use of this meditation helps us clear out emotional baggage and issues that come up from time to time.

We call ourselves to center, ground, and alignment with the Light. We call in the Four Sacred directions and the Four Elements in the name of Archangels Raphael, Michael, Gabriel, and Uriel. We choose the appropriate issues that are affecting our life that come up in meditation and release them to the Light. We honor our relationship with Spirit and release issues in peace and Love.

Meditation with the Qabalah TREE OF LIFE and the Qabalah Cross offers a way to get in touch with subconscious issues and issues from belief systems that no longer serve us—some that we may even be unaware of, though they are affecting our lives. This process of releasing emotional baggage and mental patterns and beliefs, clears our energy field to raise our vibration rate for expansion, growth, and service.

Using this meditation with the Qabalah TREE OF LIFE brings energy through our chakras that automatically brings these issues to the surface for release, consequently we need to prepare our physical bodies and mindset for such intense transformation and processing by caring for our health and

152

well-being prior to and during such a transformational exercise.

Our clearing and healing are for ourselves and the right groups that are guided to come together. The Qabalah TREE OF LIFE is about the flow of Light and steps for manifesting, starting from God most High and following teaching and initiations descending to planet Earth.

Not everyone is attracted to Qabalah. Usually, the attraction is for those with religious background using ceremony and working with the Ascended Masters and the spiritual hierarchy in service to humankind.

Meditation in a group setting is still about our personal connection, growth, and service to the Light. It is all about our expansion of consciousness and growth in awareness.

Our personal growth in consciousness adds to the growth in group consciousness.

"This is a higher spiritual truth that we are eternal beings and that our essence continues to live on in Spirit."

- John Pollock

CHAPTER XVI — CHRIST THE DOVE

Lord Jesus Christ is the Messiah!

John 11:25,26

Jesus said unto Martha, I am the resurrection, and the life: he that believeth in me, though he were dead, yet shall he live, And whosoever liveth and believeth in me shall never die.

We have already discussed in *Prayers for All Occasions* and *MYSTIC* that when Lord Jesus Christ was baptized by John the Baptist, a dove appeared above His head. I understand that Christ was grounding the Holy Spirit to Earth for the benefit of humankind.

The Holy Spirit is a bright glistening Gold Light that all humanity has access to by simply asking in meditation. Sincerity, purity of heart, and putting Christ first are the keys, and then our prayers are answered by a loving Father.

The subtle electric energies of the Holy Spirit come with the tremendous Christ consciousness of Jesus the Christ, the Son of God, having walked the Earth, performed the miracles, and ascended into Light as living proof of life hereafter for humankind. How else would humanity know that there is life in higher dimensions beyond the physical plane?

This is a higher spiritual truth that we are eternal beings and that our essence continues to live on in Spirit. Confirmation is always forthcoming.

Christ Holy Spirit touches our hearts with a sweet, strong energy blessing that is balanced masculine force of forgiveness combined with gentle and soft feminine support and acceptance. The Energy of the Dove is especially strong yet gentle for healing and miracles and bringing grace into our lives, and peace. When the Energy of the Dove is used for healing, blessings tend to be a permanent and complete healing of our whole self without reversal of the healing later.

When I received my awakening, I asked Spirit what energies I should use for healing work. I received inspiration, an intuitive voice from Spirit said that I should use the "Energy of the Dove." I discovered that when Christ was baptized by John the Baptist, the dove that appeared above their heads symbolized the anchoring of the Holy Spirit to Earth by Christ for the benefit of humankind.

Upon acceptance, humankind would have access to the Holy Spirit and the energetic connection with Jesus Christ for healing, meditation, and His teaching. This is the gift of salvation. It is a blessing and a gift to humankind to save our eternal soul and take us into heavenly bliss.

This is our access into the higher Light of God. If we ask for the Energy of the Dove with Christ, it will come to us and we are blessed in the Light and Christ Holy Spirit.

Humankind knows Christ as God incarnate as the Son of God. Christ reportedly told His disciples, "If you want to see what God looks like, look at me!"

Christ said the most important commandment for humanity to follow was to "Love the Lord thy God with all thy heart, and all thy soul, and all thy mind." Quote from the Holy Bible KJV 22:37.

23rd psalm – (faith and steadfast support) A Psalm of David:

> The LORD *is* my shepherd; I shall not want.
>
> He maketh me to lie down in green pastures: he leadeth me beside the still waters.
>
> He restoreth my soul: he leadeth me in the paths of righteousness for his name's sake.
>
> Yea, though I walk through the valley of the shadow of death, I will fear no evil: for thou *art* with me; thy rod and thy staff they comfort me.
>
> Thou preparest a table before me in the presence of mine enemies: thou anointest my head with oil; my cup runneth over.
>
> Surely goodness and mercy shall follow me all the days of my life: and I will dwell in the house of the LORD forever.

The Lord's Prayer

Our Father who art in heaven, hallowed be thy name.
Thy kingdom come. Thy will be done on earth as it is in heaven.
Give us this day our daily bread, and forgive us our trespasses,
as we forgive those who trespass against us,
and lead us not into temptation, but deliver us from evil.
For thine is the kingdom and the power, and the glory, forever and
ever. Amen.

The Lord's Prayer is good to say at night before going to sleep. Holy Mother Mary said to pray the rosary.

"Our acceptance and expression of Love is the key to grace, prosperity, giving, and receiving."

- John Pollock

CHAPTER XVII — LIVING IN LIGHT

Living in Light brings us the experience of love, wisdom, peace, harmony, and joy. Being open to these enLIGHTenments allows us to receive both forgiveness and acceptance.

Higher wisdom brings higher understanding to life, higher insight, clarity, creativity, balance, and inspiration.

Balance brings common sense and practicality into the physical world. A desire to help others does return to us in the course of our everyday life. It spontaneously comes to us in our flow.

Balance brings Divine timing and order, along with spiritual guidance. Spirit energy blends with us, and works for the highest and best for everyone involved. Our acceptance and expression of Love is the key to grace, prosperity, giving, and receiving.

There is a Norse prayer that accompanies the runes:

"I will that thy will be my will."

We surrender our will to the will of God, and use discernment over expression of our truth.

Archangel Michael helps us to express the higher purpose of Light through our personal truth within our heart and in our expression of life. He always works with our permission so as not to interfere with our free will.

Establishing a Sacred Space in prayer inherently brings protection in that our higher truth and expression is what we live. Our energy field and consciousness hold a sacred space of buoyancy that does not allow a lesser truth to come through us.

Spirit always comes with a subtle vibration of moving bio-electric energy, combined with a magnetic resonance of consciousness and higher intelligence, plus inspiration of Light in all dimensions for the best possible expression. It expands and empowers our highest choices and lifts up our lives. Spirit always comes with peace, joy, and harmony.

Light always follows our positive intention and positive expression of Love from within our heart.

This involves living in the present, expressing unconditional love, and letting go of attachments to outcomes, without getting caught up in the past or dreams of fantasy for the future.

This means maintaining faith and trust in the process that is invisible to the naked eye. We ask that Light be moving through prayer to support our lives, to evolve into miracles, and to make answers appear when we need and want them. We ask for the gift of discernment to bring confirmation, guiding our journey.

Our motivation for a win-win solution to our prayers is paramount. It is for us to follow through with our inspiration and guidance—not to follow the pipe dreams of glamour from the physical plane but to always leave room for acceptance of blessings and miracles to appear.

Visualization to Release Emotional Baggage

We envision ourselves taking off in an air balloon on our spiritual and life's journey. Bags of sand have been holding the balloon on the ground until time for take-off. As we begin our journey, we see ourselves rising higher in the multicolored balloon.

We can liken our heaviness of issues and emotional baggage in life to the sand bags weighing us down in the balloon.

We can then visualize ourselves cutting holes in the bags of sand and the sand beginning to pour out. As the sand pours out, we feel the emotional heaviness that we're holding onto begin to release and fall out with the sand, and notice that we are feeling lighter as the balloon rises higher. As a result, we feel lighter on our spiritual adventure of life.

Releasing fear of survival and the issues of power and struggle, and romance in the physical plane, is a matter of aligning with all levels of Light, starting with our inner truth and extending up through soul and Higher self, Divine Father and Mother God, to the purest heart of all creation, and All That Is. Grounding in nurturing, support, and balance with Spirit, empowers us through alignment with the Light and lifts our consciousness to higher levels and a higher flow in the physical world.

Living in Light involves transcending the issues of the physical world, putting our faith in alignment with the buoyancy of our soul consciousness. We learn to trust our guidance and our direction from Spirit to move us forward. We receive confirmation as synchronicities in our life's flow and through the miracles that come into our lives. The more we meditate with Light, the more Light we carry in our energy field. Our soul essence becomes lighter. We become closer to God.

"Aligning our life with our soul's purpose automatically brings forth joy and grace and stability."

- John Pollock

Chapter XVIII — Healing Session

All spiritual work is done through prayer. We can go to a prayer circle that is set up as a Native American Medicine Wheel vortex. The first step in any healing session is to clear our energy field and aura with energies of the Archangels, guides, and by infusing Light.

We call forth our truth from within our heart. The teaching experience is to call all chakras into alignment with our truth within our heart, Soul, and Higher Self, Divine Father and Mother God, to the Purest heart of Love and Light of all creation, and "All That Is."

We call ourselves to ground for nurturing, support, and to stabilize our energies. We call for balance between the spiritual and physical, and for empowerment in the physical world through alignment with Light.

This creates a sacred space that inherently brings protection and is ideal for clearing out negative entities and unfriendly extra-terrestrials, and such. We anchor a medicine wheel flow of energies within us, raising our vibration rate and infusing Light into our truth.

We call in the four Cardinal Directions of Air, Fire, Water, and Earth in the names of Archangels Raphael, Michael, Gabriel, and Uriel. We feel the tremendous strength of the four elemental energies hosted by the energies of the four Archangels: *Raphael*—Emerald Green for truth and healing, *Michael*—Neon Blue for empowerment and inspiration from Holy Spirit, *Gabriel*—White for purity and energies of inner and outer communication, and *Uriel*—Angel with the fiery hair and Yellow energies of wisdom and spirit activation.

The next step is to visualize an energetic medicine wheel around us, coming in from the four Cardinal Directions of East, South, West, and North, moving in a clockwise direction, and then turning to move downward through the center into Mother Earth.

As we infuse more Light into our lives, and into our living space, we are blessed in our finances, our relationships, and we are empowered through Spirit with new purpose. Our lives are lifted up. Our hearts are touched by the hand of God working in all things. Our prayers are heard and answered, and miracles are forthcoming.

Prayer

God, please show us the best possible healing and best expression in our lives.

We are the Flame of Violet Fire.
We are the purity of God!
Bless each of us, our homes, our friends, our families, our countries, our planet, our Universe.

Amen, Amen, and Amen

We know the healing.
We are the healing!

Angel on our shoulders!

This energy prayer is always made in preparation for infusing more Light, for establishing a sacred space to connect with guidance, and to establish a solid flow of Light from higher dimensions into the Earth plane. This prayer is used for spiritual healing, for meditating to receive inspiration, for putting our needs and wants out to the universe, and in programing our own Philosopher's Stone that expresses our higher purpose in alignment with our Higher Self and Spirit.

Aligning our life with our soul's purpose automatically brings forth joy and grace and stability. We experience miracles, synchronicities in our flow, and our contribution to others with ease. We receive blessings coming to us from Spirit!

These spiritual tools enhance our religious and philosophical expression and only serve to bring us closer to Spirit and our self-discovery on our own path.

"We are all healers when we choose to allow
the Light to work through us!"

- John Pollock

Chapter XIX — Flow with Light

It seems that the energies are becoming more intense in the 2020s, manifesting our dysfunction and issues that keep us off balance. Our energy fields attract our life-experiences, so it is important to meditate often to bring in Light. Light helps to dissolve impurities, and obsessive-compulsive feelings and thoughts.

It's more important than ever to realize that interactions with others are showing us stronger and stronger mirrors that we have been eliciting from our own reality. The anger and resentment toward others, that we're just sure is coming from someone else, is a manifestation of our own feelings and judgments of others.

In prayer, we ask for the Holy Spirit to bless our lives, that we may shift into a state of grace. The hardest-hitting issues that tend to repeat in our lives have value as lessons. We acknowledge those feelings to ourselves as valid feelings and allow them to pass on by. If we make the issues into a ridged block on our path that we must overcome, they become even more formidable. Our ego-personality always fights to win disagreements. Many thoughts from outside of us can become a major threat or affect us like the irritating bite from a mosquito. The difference is our perception. It is our choice to make.

A strong single focus of Love is the best. If we put out "battle energy" for our defense, we attract an even stronger adversary. The key to living in our spiritual flow is to live in the present and to turn challenges and experiences over to God. We count our blessings and appreciate miracles in our lives!

I had a great awakening in 1987 with a vision of Jesus Christ above me and Gold Light flowing through me. It was very intense. A twinkle of tiny gold stars emitted from the main stream of Gold and White Light, charging my body and flowing down to Mother Earth. I was vibrating all over. The experience stayed with me for several hours.

Days later, I awakened from yet another dream in which I was having a conversation about doing healing work. I remembered telling someone in the dream that I would like very much to facilitate healing but was uncertain about which energies I should use. The answer that came back was, "Use the Energy of the Dove." That was when I fully awakened and the conversation was over.

Some people use the energy of the Dove in healing and have a vision of a Dove at the same time. The meaning is the same.

As I was opening up to spiritual healing work, I had an interesting experience that left me with no question that the flow of Spirit was taking me on a path of learning to follow guidance and grow into healing and teaching. I had decided to travel from Denver, Colorado, to Sedona, Arizona, on a quest to meditate and experience a spiritual adventure.

The loving people in the meditation group back home set me up to connect with a woman who was divorced from a member and currently living in Sedona. This was a spiritual connection. I left Denver and drove thirteen hours to Sedona, arriving in town around five or six o'clock the next day. I called my connection and discovered there was a meeting for enlightenment that evening, so I went directly over to that meeting.

They had a great meeting. I had a strong feeling that I had something to contribute, but I was nervous about speaking. I hadn't led the group in Denver; however, I had attended many times and I knew how the meetings went.

When the meeting was over, they said goodnight and I was busting to speak. I said that in Denver, after the meditation, we would offer a healing for anyone that wanted one. They said that was ok, and asked how it was done and if I would like to lead us in that healing.

The group was still holding energy from the group meditation. I described that we would have one person at a time sit in a chair in front of the group to receive hands-on healing. I offered to do healing if anyone wanted to stay. I was surprised, nervous, and excited when *everybody* stayed. We did individual healings that night for twenty-five people. Spirit took any anxiety away and worked through me to lead a group in healing for the first time. I was to find out down the road, that Spirit always works through us to set up the learning situations in a non-threatening way. That meeting in Sedona was perfect, because nobody there knew how things were *supposed* to go, so the pressure to be perfect was off my shoulders.

I had another experience when I went to a retreat put on by another spiritual group. *Universalia* put out a newsletter and held monthly meetings promoting spirituality and unconditional Love. On one occasion, I was still new to healing work and was walking down a path through the woods going to the early evening meeting. I passed a girl walking on crutches. I stopped, not wanting to be too forward, and finally asked if she would like a Christ healing for her ankle.

She sat down and took the wrapping off her ankle and we worked and prayed for thirty minutes, or so. Afterward, I was surprised to see her pick up her wrappings and crutches, and walk off down the trail without needing them anymore.

I was still thinking over what had happened, when I came upon yet another girl with a soft cast on her ankle and also walking on crutches. I told her that we just did a healing for another girl on crutches, and I asked if she would like me to do a healing on her, as well. Afterward, I was amazed that she, too, picked up her cast and crutches and walked on down the path with no further need of them. Obviously, Spirit wanted me to know that God was working through me and that there were no meet-ups by chance.

As interesting stories go, a neighbor of mine had a refrigerator go out. In the past we'd always gone to a resale store to replace appliances. We headed off to get a replacement. The first replacement had to be returned, as it was not cold enough. The second had to be returned for the same reason. Another friend suggested we go to a used appliance store. I was praying to find a good refrigerator. Spirit was getting the message to me. While looking at Home Depot and Lowes, yet another friend was receiving inspiration. She saw in a vision the name and location of the used appliance store to go visit. It was there that we finally found a good refrigerator at a reasonable price, with a six-month guarantee.

In another appliance story, I called several stores to find a repairman who would fix our dishwasher. The repairman cancelled an appointment, as he had an accident and couldn't come.

The next repairman set an appointment, but in the meantime, the washing machine went out in the basement. The repairman found nothing wrong with the dishwasher, but found that the washing machine needed to be replaced. I had been storing a Maytag washer and dryer in the garage for several years. Long story short, we found the right people to swap out the washing machines and everything fell into place.

This next story took place in Sedona, Arizona, many years ago. I had driven up from Phoenix to meet three other people. We had planned to do a ceremony together in a medicine wheel. When I arrived in Sedona, the other three people were all taking some other detour with their activities. I connected with a spiritual buddy, and then decided to do a medicine wheel by myself.

I found a good spot off the trail, and I started doing prayers. One by one, three other people showed up and wanted to know if they could join in the medicine wheel ceremony. The experience was highly spiritual and better than what I had originally planned.

I had yet another unusual experience when connecting with a spiritual friend in Sedona before getting ready to do a medicine wheel. Sol and I were visiting and sharing experiences, when I realized, on that hot afternoon on the porch, that there was a multitude of flies buzzing around us. Spirit was definitely with us. All of a sudden, I was moved to proclaim to the flies, "If you want to live, leave now!" There was complete silence and the flies were suddenly gone. Sol and I were looking into each other's eyes. Our mouths dropped open, but no flies flew in.

While I was living in Sedona, a man came by my Angels Grace healing center. He came down the street to tell me about a message he had received for me. He was guided to tell me that I needed to clear my crystals. I didn't know him, and although I am usually leery of messages from strangers, this seemed to ring true and resonate with me. Spirit always finds a way to get in touch. We ask the Holy Spirit for the gift of discernment to recognize truth coming to us.

Many years ago, while I was working in my healing booth at a fair, a friend received a message that Saint Germain asked if he could bless my crystal that was anchoring Light at the booth. Of course, that was okay!

So many spiritual experiences! Another was during a metaphysical fair held in Colorado Springs, Colorado. I had a very good friend whom I would accompany to the fair. I went to her house to travel together, and we stopped by her mom's house along the journey. There, we found that her mom was hurting badly from rheumatoid arthritis, and I offered a prayer for healing. During the prayer, I was concentrating on putting Light into her hand, and the field of Light around her collapsed into the palm of her hand. My friend came into the living room and felt the energetic shift, questioning what had happened. She always held a Sacred Space for her mom.

At the end of the last day at that fair, my friend had heard from her mom, who told her that her hand was completely healed. She said, "If I knew that was going to happen, I would have asked for my whole body to be healed!"

Asking for guidance and for healing from Spirit always brings answers through prayer, although God answers prayer in His own way, in His own timing.

The past experiences written here were all synchronistic, as were many, many others. They are representative of my spiritual quest and gifts from Spirit. We plant seeds for manifesting our needs and desires by releasing our prayers to the Universe.

We are all healers when we choose to allow the Light to work through us!

"Gnosis is the process of recognizing the spark of God that resides within each of us in humanity."

- John Pollock

CHAPTER XX — SPIRIT TEACHINGS

Initiations instill spiritual wisdom and charge the aura in preparation for further work on higher spiritual levels. Irving Feurst, in his work with the Hathors, offers two major initiations to begin working with star systems and the masters, providing nine further initiations for spiritual advancement. The first is an initiation to fortify the energy field, and the second is the anti-glamour initiation to give clarity to situations and issues that come up in the illusions arising on the physical plane.

We call in the four cardinal directions with elemental energies, combining powerful elemental energies of Air,

Fire, Water, and Earth to work together to form a sacred chalice, anchoring Light coming into our sacred prayer circle. We surround ourselves with Light for inspiration and higher energies to carry out our spiritual work.

This ability to energetically program our lives in prayer, and take our spiritual vision up to soul, was given to humanity over ten thousand years ago by Hermes Thrice-Great Trismegistus. He referred to this as energetically creating our personal Philosopher's Stone to empower our spiritual purpose and our life-expression. We experience the energies of our soul as a solid connection that remains constant in support of our life-expression and allows for the influx of Light from higher dimensions, bringing in our higher soul's purpose with guidance to manifest our best.

Our prayer involves rising up to the Mind of God in our imagination and bringing Fire energies down to lower dimensions to be expressed in the physical. This was the basis of the Gnostic Gospels—the use of a process known as alchemy for healing and expansion in consciousness.

"Gnosis" is the process of recognizing the spark of God that resides within each of us in humanity. This spark was given to us upon our incarnation in a physical body, enabling life on the physical plane. We each come with this spark of God within, and Hermes tells us that we would be well-served to meditate to bring the Fire energies from Mind, Source God, to set our individual spark ablaze.

Our spark inside will flare up with Light and higher consciousness and expand our relationship with God and creation. This process is given to us in the Gnostic Gospels, and includes the wisdom given to us by Hermes in the *Emerald Tablet* and several handwritten ancient scrolls, setting forth the basis for the development of alchemy and expansion of consciousness.

Further information on the process of alchemy and the Gnostic Gospels burning away self-deception and illusion, can be found in my first two books, *Prayers* and *MYSTIC*. This includes the dissolution of heaviness to remove emotional baggage and pain in soul-energy.

This is the ancient path to enlightenment given by Hermes Thrice-Great Trismegistus, and it is covered in great detail in my book, *MYSTIC: Manifesting Your Soul, Truth in Consciousness.* This information was put forth to humankind by Hermes in a document called "The Corpus Hermeticum" and Hermetic tradition. There is another book written by three un-named initiates that offers the teachings of Hermes Thrice-Great for further research. It is called the "Kybalion."

In our spiritual worship set forth along with The *Emerald Tablet,* we are reminded of the importance of the practice of meditation and the nature of higher consciousness. The practice of prayer and meditation to activate Light within was brought forth by Hermes. His teaching was to help each individual to re-discover their own path of enlightenment and to make their own soul-journey to the Light.

Concerning The Corpus Hermeticum

Hermes channeled the Divine Mind of God to understand the structure of creation. It was revealed to Hermes that all creation is structured with levels of consciousness within levels of consciousness. Each level is a step down in vibration on its way to the creation of Earth and humanity, and all things in between.

Although each level has a different function, the descent of Light is not linear. The energies are multi-dimensional. The energies of Divine Mind are constantly in motion. They are under pressure to fill all levels of consciousness within, and to fill all Souls with Light. All living things have a soul and sustain life on their particular level. The Light is constantly swirling to lower dimensions and back up to higher dimensions.

At the top is our Source Creator—the good, the beautiful, the wisdom, the blessedness. The next level down is the level of Aeon. It is sameness. It includes lastingness and deathlessness. It was formed to be the Soul to creation within and sustain all life below. Divine Mind is the energy of God. It flows between God on High and all creation below, filling all souls and sustaining all forms of life.

Presented here is that discussion between Hermes in Light-body Himself, and Divine Mind, as part of the Gnostic Gospels translated by GRS Mead.

Concerning the Secret Sermon on the Mount
(CORPUS HERMETICUM XIII)

Concerning rebirth and the promise of silence of Thrice-Great Hermes spoken to Tat his son:

Tat said to his father that he felt like his father was speaking in riddles. It was unclear how no man could ever be saved before Rebirth in Divinity. Tat wanted to understand about the Rebirth experience. Humanity feels frustration in much the same way.

Hermes said to Tat, "Whenever I see within myself the Simple Vision brought to birth out of God's mercy, I have passed through myself into a Body that can never die. And now I am not what I was before; but I am born in Mind. The way to do this is not taught, and it cannot be seen by the compounded element [sight in the physical] by means of which thou seest me."

The key is to re-make ourself and become a stranger to the world of illusion. Hermes describes the process of enlightenment to his son Tat as becoming aware of our self in the body, and then becoming aware of our self in a Lighter and more energetic body, as if standing behind our self in an eternal etheric body that never dies.

We acquire an expanded awareness with Spirit. This awareness is much like the soul-awareness we are given when working with Christ healing and teachings in meditation.

With Christ, our awareness of our own soul seems to be perceived through our Third-Eye and Crown chakras. It is our soul-consciousness, appearing like a bright, gold, sparkling energy-cloud located three feet or more above our head. Getting in touch with the feeling and sense of our soul is an effective way of reaching out to make our connection from our spiritual truth within, to Higher Self. We receive blessings from higher dimensions in prayer.

Hermes said that our spiritual essence transcends the senses and is transformed into another essence by God. He refers to this higher essence as a new "Race." When it is God's Will, the memory of Light is restored to us. We no longer have the previous sense of touch and dimension, yet we have a new sense of touch and dimension. We have new eyes with which to see, and new dimensions of Divinity to perceive. We are surrounded in a garment of Light that does not change.

We are warned against telling others that we are transformed, to avoid being accused of bragging or accused by malicious intent. We teach in sincerity to those who are ready to learn, and keep the covenant of silence in our sacred transformation.

"In sincerity, with a desire to open to the higher influence
of God and the Holy Spirit expressing through us,
we may be granted dispensation and access
to the higher Flames of Light."

- John Pollock

Chapter XXI — Angels & Holy Flames of Light

In my first book *Prayers for All Occasions,* I talked extensively about the seven Rays and their relationship to the human body, as well as their relationship to the Angels that work with each individual Ray. The Rays are each a different aspect of God, but they all have one thing in common—they are all bringing Divine Love with a specialized focus and a specific purpose, blessing humankind.

Each Ray is a body of consciousness from God, that merges with our energy field so we may learn how it feels to raise our vibration, to operate with higher wisdom, higher guidance, and to experience expressing a higher expression of our truth in accordance with the Archangel who is merging with us to help lift our spiritual essence to higher levels with God.

All Angels are in service to God. We may work with Angels that have come through us to help in teaching and healing. Archangels Raphael, Michael, Gabriel, and Uriel are the primary Archangels blending with our energies and teaching the "right" use of Light in connecting with higher dimensions of God, and the higher expression of Love and creativity on the worldly planes of existence.

The Rays bring through a spiritual perspective, sharing Love, peace, harmony, joy, and beauty resonating in all areas of our lives. The appearance of blessings from Spirit, synchronicities, and on-going miracles, are all indicators that we are on track.

Frequent meditation and prayer bring us closer to Spirit. Visualization of the color of the Rays while tuning into the desired Archangels with their attributes helps us to enhance the energy that comes through us when we make an energetic connection to the Light through many dimensions. The Archangels bless us with an energetic connection and wisdom to answer our prayers.

The Archangels bring us comfort, higher insight, and understanding, as well as assistance with empowerment through alignment in Divine Love and Light. By calling in the seven Rays and their corresponding Archangels, we merge with the higher teaching of Angels working through us and resonate with purification. Our energy fields are charged.

Archangel Michael and Lady Faith bring us strength and the power of God on the first Ray, the Neon Blue Ray. This corresponds to the Throat chakra. This power of God is not the power to control others, but the sacred empowerment of our personal truth, yet not to interfere with our own free will. We are empowered to deal with difficult situations and difficulties with others while bringing strength to our expression. When we turn our challenges over to Spirit, we gain strength, wisdom, and enlightenment.

Archangel Jofiel and Lady Constance are a liaison from soul to the Crown chakra known as the Wisdom Ray. This is the second Ray, the Gold Ray, working through meditation and trust, assisting with guidance, inspiration, and empowerment of our visions. Knowingness, discernment, and timing come together into decision-making.

Archangel Chamuel and Lady Charity bring us the third Ray, the Pink Ray of unconditional love, to bring together higher spiritual Love with love from the physical plane into our hearts, Heart chakra. We learn to appreciate the flow of higher Love into our lives. We also ask in prayer for the gift of discernment from the Holy Spirit. When we ask, the Holy

Spirit tells us in our heart whether people or situations are "right" for us, letting us know if they for our highest good to follow on our path.

Archangel Gabriel and Lady Hope bring us the fourth Ray, the White Ray of purity, working through our Base chakra life-force energy to communicate within ourselves. We also communicate on a sensory basis with the Universe on higher dimensions. This is also empowerment of our physical expression and links our physical energy fields to Spirit.

Archangel Raphael and Holy Mother Mary bring us the fifth Ray, the Emerald Green Ray of truth and healing, working through the Third-Eye chakra. False belief systems are purged and emotions are released to bring energies into balance, into a state of grace. First higher, then lower frequencies vibrate in ripples and waves, shaking out heaviness in thinking and discordant energies.

Archangel Uriel and Aurora bring in the sixth Ray, Ruby and Gold Ray of service, through the Solar Plexus chakra. They assist teachers, accountants, and lawyers, as well as spiritual teachers and healers. Jesus Christ was working on this Ray. This combines the Red Life-Force energy and Gold Wisdom, putting Spirit into action. They teach the power of Truth and Love over fear.

Archangel Tzadkiel and Lady Amethyst work through the Spleen or Sacral chakra. This is the seventh Ray, the Violet Ray of Transformation. It combines the first three Rays: the Neon Blue Ray for Power of God, the Gold Ray for Wisdom of God, and the Pink Ray for Unconditional Love. Together they form the Violet Threefold Flame that resides in the heart. The Violet Ray works to clear discordance, release judgment, and bring new possibilities forward. Saint Germain is an Ascended Master. He uses the Violet Light to balance karma with affirmations and decrees. This is all about releasing energies that restrict our spiritual essence, expanding Light, and experiencing new freedom and creativity.

The Holy Flames of Light

The Angels tell us that the Holy Flames were originally given to humankind, bringing the spiritual power of God to help raise our vibration rate and our state of consciousness.

Upon incarnating on the physical plane, our spiritual essence underwent a process of involution, where vibrations were slowed down and we took on a lower consciousness in order to experience many aspects of love and to better learn the spiritual lessons of the lower dimensions on Earth.

As our soul incorporates lessons and experience from Earth, our spiritual essence quickens and our vibration increases in a process known as evolution. Humankind experiences transcendence of the lower realms and a merging of consciousness with that of higher consciousness, Spirit.

The energies of the Holy Flames of Light are much higher than the Rays. They are an extension into even higher dimensions of Spirit—expressions of the purity of God with the purpose of raising awareness and lifting us up to rejoin our creator God on our spiritual journey home. Our male and female energies of the physical are combined for our higher expression in Spirit.

The bringing of the Holy Flames of Light to humanity were well-intended. They were meant to provide substantial assistance from God to help humankind transcend lower issues of fear and survival, releasing need of power over others, and reaching enlightened understanding of Love.

The Angels tell us that the power of the Flames was misused. We were not meant to get caught up in the glamour of worldly drama. There were people who used the energies and the power of the Flames for their own ends, for wealth, for control, for advantage over others. The Holy Flames were meant for freedom and empowerment with Spirit.

Spirit withdrew the power of the Holy Flames until they could be used with guidance, with spiritual purpose, and in accordance with the Light. There was one exception—Saint Germain made compelling arguments on behalf of humankind to let him oversee the Violet Transmuting Flame, also known as the Violet Threefold Flame.

The Violet Transmuting Flame has the Blue Ray of Archangel Michael and Lady Faith woven together with the Gold Ray of Archangel Jofiel and Lady Constance, and combined with the Pink Ray of Archangel Chamuel and Lady Charity. This combines the strength and power of God with the wisdom of God and the unconditional love of God. This is used in prayer and invocation with Saint Germain for the transformation of humankind.

Invocation to Archangel Tzadkiel and Lady Amethyst, and to Saint Germain overseeing the Violet Transmuting Flame, cuts through the dimensions with a medicine wheel vortex leading to Source, bringing in the purity and power of God and anchoring it through our heart intention In prayer and into ground below.

A simple invocation would be:

I am the Flame of Violet Fire,
I am the Purity of God,
I am the expression of electromagnetic spirit
I am the buoyancy of Violet Light,
I am the Blazing Light of God's will
Perfect expression is expanding and creating through me!

Amen, Amen, and Amen

A good friend and associate of mine was driving on a highway southwest of Denver one night when she could suddenly feel and see a very high electric energy running like a river along both sides of the highway. She recognized that it was a very fine expression of Violet Light.

The area through which she had been driving had once been a sacred site of Native American holy prayer and ceremony. There were no settlements of people back then and few still to detract from the sacred prayers. Without issues from Earth-plane humanity, it would seem the prayers have been holding a sacred connection to Violet Light flowing into the area. A vortex had likely been created with repeated prayer, and Light is still being continually infused.

Saint Germain teaches us that using invocations and affirmations raise both our vibration and our consciousness by bringing in the Violet Flame of Transformation. The use of spiritual prayer gives us the tools to getting centered and grounded and aligned with the Light within our heart, to our Soul and Higher Self, higher dimensions of Spirit, and to ground. We also call in the four cardinal directions. With an infusion of higher Violet Light, we come into alignment within ourselves.

To use the Violet Flame for transformation is much the same as using the alchemy of Hermes of over ten thousand years ago. We use the same techniques when we have physical afflictions, or when we have emotional issues of feeling "less than" when worrying about being controlled by others, fearing threats, issues of survival, being caught up in the glamour of worldly drama, and others. Most physical afflictions have underlying emotional issues attached that must be resolved.

We first call in the Archangels and Saint Germain, whereas in alchemy, we call in our connection to the **ONE MIND**—Source God, and to the ONE THING—God to the physical world. Whatever issues come up, we put each issue, and the feelings around that issue, into the Violet Transmuting Flame to be dissolved and transformed. When we do this, we are stabilized and moved into grace, into the higher Light of compassion where we are open to receiving higher guidance, empowering us on our path.

In spiritual transformation, we use the higher purity and intensity of the higher Flames of Light to move our growth in alignment with guidance and express our heart flame from our truth within. The more we are aligned in right action with the higher purpose of the Holy Spirit, the more we are empowered with the higher Light of the seven Rays, and then the even higher energies of the Holy Flames of Light. When we meditate with the seven Rays, we receive inspiration about the Holy Flames of Light and their teaching.

In sincerity, with a desire to open to the higher influence of God and the Holy Spirit expressing through us, we may be granted dispensation and access to the higher Flames of Light. When we are in alignment with our higher purpose, in right action, we begin merging with the embodiment of the Holy Spirit.

We may experience the higher empowerment and protection of the sacred Neon Blue Flame of Archangel Michael. We may receive higher wisdom and guidance from the Gold Wisdom Flame moving through us on our path. We may become, more deeply, the spiritual expression and creativity of the Pink Flame of unconditional Love. We may experience and better understand the purity of our spiritual essence and our communication with the Light.

We may know our spiritual purpose better and see our service more clearly. All humankind may call in Ascended Master Saint Germain to release heavy emotional issues, afflictions, and challenging situations into the blazing Violet Flame. Light is shining Love and empowerment. It is expanding through our consciousness and through our lives. Deeper core issues become available to be addressed.

It is good to know that the spark of Light within every person, which enables us to embody our spiritual essence in physical form, is a smaller version of the structure of creation. The spark of light within us is also called our "Heart Flame."

In the large view, the Eternal Flame of God is the eternal, never-ending consciousness and energetic expression of Mind, our Source God. It encompasses and fuels all of creation. It is for every person to discover individually where we fit and what our expanding consciousness is showing us about the world reality we live in, and about ourselves.

"The Mind of God contains all thoughts in creation."

- John Pollock

CHAPTER XXII — AWAKENING

Christ Holy Spirit

My epiphany and spiritual awakening is described in the preface to my first book *Prayers for All Occasions*. Everyone has their own individual experiences, yet Spirit always makes itself known to us in a way that we can each understand.

When we are ready to receive, and when we are searching for answers in our own lives, God Blesses us with initiation of Light. It is frequently experienced through our energetic *emotional* body, expanding our energy field, and bringing new awareness into our feminine side *feeling* body.

Our feminine side—*receiving consciousness*—is the doorway to enlightenment that is often referred to as our being "Born Again" to our Higher Spiritual essence, which is our eternal self with God, and which never dies.

Before my awakening, I was dealing with chaos and confusion in my life. I was praying for change quite often and going to several meditation groups every week, searching for revelation and higher understanding. I wanted to bring grace into my life and empowerment into my spiritual path, not really knowing where I was headed with certainty or what it would be like when I got there.

Wherever I was in the world, in each meditation group, there were always several facilitators that would lead us in prayer. On one auspicious occasion in April of 1987, several leaders facilitated prayer in Lakewood, Colorado, and the group energies again rose. The Christ Light funneled through several leaders in service to the Light and blessed me. I could feel the high energies in my personal energy field as it expanded. I could also see sparkling gold Light swirling around me.

I could feel everything that was going on and see it all through my Third-Eye chakra, like a clear dream-vision. Lord Jesus Christ had appeared above me with extended arms.

An intense White Light came through Christ and was slowly trickling down through my head and gradually moving through my entire body. There was also a sparkling gold light circling the room.

The whole experience was so bizarre. I could see in multiple dimensions at the same time. I could see Light coming down to me from Christ above, and coming into me. At the same time, it was as if I was above it all, watching the Light descending from the heavens, moving through Christ and through me.

This experience was totally unexpected and amazing. Who could imagine such an event blessing our life? What's even more surprising is that after going to the Light, miracles begin to flow through us. We are blessed, others are blessed! Prayers are empowered by Spirit, and they bring higher energy to our energy field.

Prayer always begins with centering and getting grounded. Self-mastery is a matter of aligning with the Light, surrendering to God, and flowing with guidance as the Light lifts us up.

Since this miracle healing, I have meditated every day, as well as once a week in group, to stay aligned with the Light and stabilize in my emotions and energy field. The weekly meeting is for manifesting needs and desires on our path. Everyone supports everyone else in the group and all humanity.

In addition to prayers at the time of my awakening with Christ, Angels, and Holy Spirit, I have since included the practice of establishing a Sacred Space using the Native

American Medicine Wheel technique for infusing Light on Earth.

In the name of the Archangels, we invoke the Sacred elemental energies of the four cardinal directions. We call to Archangel Raphael in the direction of Air from the East, to Archangel Michael in the direction of Fire from the South, to Archangel Gabriel in the direction of Water from the West, and to Archangel Uriel in the direction of Earth from the North. This creates a chalice to hold Higher Light anchored through us and to Mother Earth.

We call Saint Germain forward to work in a similar way as the alchemy of Hermes Trismegistus that was taught ten thousand years before. We call Saint Germain forward to consume negativity, to raise the vibration of our lives, and to teach us self-mastery in our spiritual journey. We put difficult life-situations into the Violet Flame with Saint Germain to flash-incinerate problems and bring higher consciousness to bear.

Hermes Trismegistus

Ten thousand years ago, Hermes Thrice-Great Trismegistus wrote in the Gnostic Gospels, introducing a process he described as *meditating* to be reborn in Spirit. Reaching up in spiritual imagination, we merge with Source Mind of God, and bring the intense energies down to combine with the ONE THING which empowers the God of our solar system. The ONE THING is the level of God-consciousness that we on Earth identify as "God" to whom the different religions in humanity pray.

The Mind of God contains all thoughts in creation. As fire energies descend, they join with all feelings and emotions contained in the ONE THING, providing humanity with answers to our prayers.

This ONE THING is the level of consciousness on Earth that we understand as God, that the various religions pray to reach in their religious ceremonies and from whom our prayers seek answers in our everyday lives. This is the same level of consciousness that Hermes speaks of in the *Emerald Tablet*.

Hermes spoke in the Gnostic Gospels, Volume 2, in the *Secret Sermon on the Mountain,* a written dissertation to his son, Tat, concerning rebirth of the spiritual essence of humankind and a promise of Sacred Light in silence.

Tat asks the question of Hermes, and humanity now asks how humankind is reborn in Spirit? It is a matter of transcending the essence and transcending the senses from those of the physical embodiment into a new set of senses with Spirit in a new embodiment in God, and into a higher dimension.

This does not take place through Earth-level vision and learning, but rather through the mercy of God and by God's will. It happens when we find a quiet space within and put the outward physical senses of the body out of work. Our Divinity comes forward. We *will* it to come forward. When we *will* that we are reborn in God, it comes to pass. We have passed through ourselves into a body that can never die. We are not what we were before; we are reborn in Mind. It is as if we are now standing above and behind ourselves with a new vision and perspective.

In this process, the torments of the physical life, numbering twelve or more, are dissolved. Not-knowing, grief, intemperance, concupiscence, unrighteousness, avarice, error, envy, guile, anger, resentment, judgment, rashness, and malice—all dissolved.

The powers of God in Gnosis and purification bring joy, self-control, power against desire, righteousness, truth, the good, the life, the Light—darkness has vanquished!

This knowledge is not taught in ordinary life teachings, and is not comprehended by the ordinary mind, but is kept hidden in Sacred silence where God bestows it upon us.

PRAISE GOD, THE EYE OF MIND!
BE STILL!

The Emerald Tablet

The ancient wisdom and teaching from Hermes in the *Emerald Tablet* concerns the expression "As Above, So Below," which refers to our understanding of Higher consciousness and how it relates to consciousness here on the Earth plane.

All creation is a manifestation or adaptation of the ONE THING. The ONE THING is the consciousness of God that governs the physical plane. The force of the ONE THING penetrates every subtle thing and every solid thing in creation.

Hermes identified himself as the author of the *Emerald Tablet*. He said, "I am called Hermes Trismegistus, having the three parts of the philosophy of the whole world.

"The First Part is SPIRIT, the Sun, which is our rational, masculine nature,

"The Second Part is CONSCIOUSNESS, soul, which is our unseen connection to God,

"The Third Part is FORM, the Moon, our irrational, intuitive and feminine nature."

Hermes tells us that all things that happen on Earth can be understood as a combination of these influences on the Earth plane.

Hermes teaches meditation to anchor Light with the four cardinal directions and the elemental Earth energies. He teaches reaching up to our highest source God-Mind, and bringing the rarified energies down to merge with the ONE THING which governs the physical plane.

He tells us to put forth to the universe our soul's purpose in prayer. Our spiritual essence expands. We ask for order and empowerment for our spiritual path, and grace in our physical life. He refers to putting our physical life into living prayer as the Philosopher's Stone, which brings our intention into manifestation of our spiritual path through our physical expression.

The process of transformation involves calling our fears, anger, grief, and issues from the physical world, to be flash-burned and dissolved in the Light. This explosive release of heaviness from our spiritual essence is referred to as the process of alchemy raising up our vibration. We release into fire our mental patterns from reactive mind and emotions to be replaced with higher love and empowerment through Light.

Ancient Wisdom

The Qabalah TREE OF LIFE is a teaching that was given by God to Humanity through the Hebrews. It is said to be a diagram, or glyph, that is a projection from the Mind of God. God "thinks" the TREE OF LIFE into being to teach humankind about the stepping down in consciousness and the lowering in vibration rate that we experience, as Light descends in its support of humankind in the physical.

The TREE OF LIFE is a teaching about higher dimensions of God and initiations in higher consciousness that we experience, first in higher realms, then along the way as Light makes its way down towards physical expression through us.

We have discussed the TREE OF LIFE in great detail in *Prayers for All Occasions,* and *MYSTIC: Manifesting Your Soul, Truth in Consciousness.*

To summarize, Light descends through the TREE OF LIFE in a lightning bolt pattern toward Earth. The roots of the Tree are in Heaven. The TREE is seen as our path of evolution on each of four levels, or four "worlds." The highest is EMANATION; next is the world of CREATION; then comes FORMATION; and finally, the world of ACTION. There are four worlds with the bottom of one TREE OF LIFE being the top of the next TREE OF LIFE below.

Meditation is always carried out in balance with work performed on one pillar, it is always accompanied by work on the opposite pillar. This maintains balanced polarity and stability in our life.

Appropriate spiritual life lessons are learned in experiencing the Light at one sephira level after another. Initiations bring new awareness and insights.

In meditating to receive insight on our lives, we can receive a charge in our energy field and wisdom to apply to our lives and in solving situations we are dealing with.

Meditating with the Qabalah Cross Meditation Is a powerful way to tap into consciousness of the TREE OF LIFE in one meditation to activate the energies at all levels of our lives. We can access insights, and new awareness affecting mental issues and emotional blockages. The energies of Light move through our energy field with a woosh, moving our consciousness forward in a hurry!

Regardless of our religious or cultural conditioning, Awakening comes to us on a cellular level when we connect directly with Spirit Source God, either in solitude or in a group. Meditation is a key to unlock all doors in this direction.

"Sound and meditation lift us out of lower issues in the Earth plane, and take us to greater intimacy in prayer, transcending lower consciousness."

- John Pollock

Chapter XXIII — *SHIFT!*

Everything is energy. Energy always carries consciousness with it. In God's work to create our universe and our dear planet Earth, He has created from His unlimited consciousness and wisdom, and His never-ending Love and Light. God has created humankind with a spark of God-Light inside each person. This spark of God-Light endows each of us with empowerment for our prayers and inspiration for manifestation of our life path.

This is our opportunity to experience creating on our own from our God-given free will, just as our creator instantly manifests the thoughts from the Mind of God into existence.

This happens through magnetic attraction. Our intention focuses our life force energy to attract manifestation of our needs and desires. Our Heart Flame attracts the teachers we are looking for, new friends of shared spiritual purpose, and opportunities with best direction moving along our life path.

The drama and adventure that play out in our lives are the reflections of the positive and negative states of our truth within and our connection with Light flowing through us. Intimacy with Spirit leads to greater intimacy in personal relationships and a more fulfilling life.

Peace, joy, positive expectation in Light, and prayer for the highest and best for everyone, brings miracles and synchronicities into our flow of Light. We put our life-circumstances into the Light. Abandonment and non-acceptance are released. Selfishness is released.

Gain at other people's expense would only give us temporary advantage with karmic repercussions. We have a knowingness that prosperity and plenty is here for everyone. That is when the economy flourishes, civilizations grow, and we are all blessed in the Light.

The Hathors describe themselves as a civilization that ascended together in ancient Egypt. They came ahead of us to teach and to assist, but not to interfere with the spiritual path of evolution of other civilizations in humanity. The Goddess Hathor was known as the Goddess of Love. She was worshipped for two thousand years, up until the Goddess Isis came into prominence.

The Hathors were able to ascend as a civilization numbering one million participants or more. The Hathors teach us to use sacred geometry with voice and sound vibration in meditation to raise the energy level of each chakra to a higher level of spiritual expression through unconditional love. Each person must do his or her own consciousness engineering. Taken as a whole, the result is to raise group consciousness for all of humanity. A grasping love with jealously and selfish desires is raised to a more unconditional Love and becomes a win-win for all. Expression on all levels can be lifted to be a representation of the purpose of the Holy Spirit.

Our baser instincts can be raised to a higher expression of Love. The Angels tell us that their purpose here is not to serve the desires of humankind, but rather to assist humankind in *overcoming* their own desires. Humankind is assisted by the Angels, Beings of Light, and the Ascended Masters in raising our consciousness, promoting growth, and assisting our evolution in the Light.

The first indication of awakening after the experience itself, is when attending a spiritual fair, business gathering, or social event, we become aware that we have attracted certain energies of like individuals drawn together for a higher spiritual purpose. This also applies to having attracted personal friendships and romantic relationships.

We are told that *A Course in Miracles* is channeled inspiration from Lord Jesus Christ. Christ tells us that, at first, we are attracted to a partner through energetic chemistry and attraction, but for a romantic or personal relationship to last, it must evolve toward the purpose of the Holy Spirit. This gives us a glimpse of the rising of energies that are lifting us through the duality in evolution here on planet Earth.

Our evolutionary growth happens in stages, just as for each individual, so also for the whole. Humankind has just entered the stage, or "age," of cosmic-consciousness Aquarius, estimated to be here for one thousand years to come. Just as we have our own flow, we are also a part of humanity's flow. People coming and going through our lives are also in this process of transcendence being guided by Spirit.

One night, I was attending a group in prayer that was based in *A Course in Miracles*. That evening, a woman came to the group meeting in search of spiritual help in her life. She was not a regular member of the group. The leader of the prayer group called me aside to work with her in individual healing.

Her story sounded impossible to solve. She owed way too much money, had three kids, and was unable to make ends meet working three jobs. She was exhausted and looking for answers.

My first response was to rack my brain and ask Spirit for answers to give her. It didn't seem like there was any solution. Then we were guided to pray together and turn everything over to Christ Holy Spirit. Our prayer lifted her spirits, and she left in a state of peace.

After she left, I realized that she must have been guided to come to our meeting that night, and Spirit was working through me to get a healing to her. Spirit was working through everyone necessary to get the job done.

This was an example of the rising consciousness and energies that will be guiding humanity with the evolution of Light in times to come. Her sincerity and Love made her one with the Light. We trust that the Light is still guiding her after that night of healing.

Recently, I had a visit from a dear friend who helps me with house cleaning and other work that I can't easily do myself. Her schedule opened up on a Saturday morning. She called and confirmed that it was a good time to come. Afterward, she and I went out for lunch and had a nice visit.

Just as we were leaving to return home, she received a phone call from a friend who had another friend needing assistance in a hospital close by. Once back at home, she and I lit a candle and said a prayer for her two friends. She then left to visit them in the hospital.

Everything had come together according to a higher plan from Spirit. It was then that I realized this, too, was an example of the synchronicities of the Light moving in concert through many people to accomplish a higher purpose.

In the past, humanity has grown accustomed to viewing ourselves through a consciousness of duality. With duality, all things are black or white, hot or cold, tall or short, loving or threatening, spiritual or physical, empowered or unempowered. Individuals strive to achieve success for themselves, yet feel that they are separate from everyone else. Their challenge has been to let go of selfishness, and understand that prosperity is here for all. Through praying for everyone, we open the doors for success and love to come to ourselves, as well. Love is the only thing that increases, coming to us by giving more away.

Prayer has been the common bridge from humanity to higher consciousness and higher vibration. As we begin to move into the Aquarian age, our Love, our intention, and our prayers of good will, begin to raise our awareness and take us into a common union with Spirit. The omnipotence of God, the wisdom, and the higher intelligence, all reach down to guide and bless each of us on our individual path, along with the highest spiritual interworkings through Light work for the common good of all, touching all humanity.

As with answers to individual prayer, the Light is now beginning to answer prayers for everyone simultaneously at higher dimensions of Light, from a common union of consciousness and higher level of synchronicity. The Light is blending the illusion of separateness by interconnecting our intuition and sensitivity of humanity on a grand scale. Polarities still form the basis of creation, yet they are reconciled by grace and provide greater understanding.

The old paradigm was called a carbon-based reality with understanding that Light is raised in consciousness in a never-ending spiral recurring in nature, called a Fibonacci scale—starting from a point that is infinitesimally small, with no beginning and widening out in unlimited fashion. The new, higher consciousness is expanded as a fluid Light, touching and reaching all dimensions, and is referred to as crystalline consciousness.

We teach, we trust, and we know that we are creating from the Light within us, being mindful to project only the positive and life-affirming aspects from within ourselves that we choose to express as our life.

We release issues of anger, resentment, sadness, grief, abandonment, struggle of power and authority, all into the Light to be consumed, as these issues would only attract harsh life experiences. Mass consciousness of humanity becomes Lighter and is lifted up.

Life is Sacred. We live in the present where we can create miracles and manifest energies of peace and fulfillment originating in the present for transformation into the future. We release holding onto drama, and stabilize our lives with prayer—bringing joy, order, and grace moving forward.

We infuse Light on a regular basis, maintaining a balance of Spirit into the physical and empowering our lives through alignment with Light.

We ask for and receive the gift of discernment from the Holy Spirit, manifesting positive feelings in our hearts as confirmation that we are receiving our own truth as guidance for our decisions and prayers on our path. The answers we receive are spiritual direction for us, and we accept that others have to follow their own guidance.

After my awakening in Spirit, I embarked on a path of healing work, learning and teaching, and tremendous expansion of awareness. I was confronted with divergent religious philosophies and the teachings of others. I was overwhelmed sorting through all the different energies, searching to discover my deeper truth.

I finally came to a great realization. For me, it was, is, and always will be much more important to distinguish between energies of Light and Dark than to get caught up in the differences between one religion and another. It was, is, and always will be more important to guide my path using Love and Light—using Christ Holy Spirit as my guide.

Be vigilant in observing that all interactions in the physical world are mirroring our inner workings within ourselves. At first, it looks like all problems are with people outside of ourselves. Outside challenges are only indications of release work for us to do, remembering that spiritual growth is an "inside job." We may not have time to work with every mirror, but we get insight on our core issues and deal with them as they come to surface for immediate attention.

The Angels tell us that God created the energetic sephirot on the TREE OF LIFE as a mirror to Himself so He can see issues within Himself in Creation.

Hermes tells us in the *Emerald Tablet* that everything in life is energy. Friendships, business relationships, spiritual relationships, and what we experience in life. All creation is made up of masculine, feminine, and spiritual energy. Our mirrors reflect to us whether we are experiencing masculine energies projecting force into our vision, or feminine energies holding the form that our creations will take.

Sometimes, when flow looks to be doing well and we are successful, yet it never seems that we are doing good enough no matter how hard we work to be fulfilled, it means that our flow is off balance to the masculine side. On the other hand, when our flow seems to work with less effort and the better it works, the better it works, we can see that our flow is balanced to the feminine side.

Prayer and spiritual energies take our energy field to a balanced place, where things work well for us and life is empowered in line with our soul path and our spiritual guidance. Most of the time, we tend to be working hard in our masculine energy to bring in business, when our feminine energy would work better to attract prosperity and a more graceful lifestyle filled with joy.

It is good to remember that our energy fields attract people with similar issues. This is the basis for us to choose spiritual counselors and healing facilitators with whom we resonate, as they have had similar experiences themselves that will help them relate to us.

With regard to close relationships, we have a tendency to enmesh with the consciousness of others and their energetic issues. This makes it difficult to tell if the issues at hand are theirs or our own, as they are often shared to a large extent. This is especially true with romantic and sexual relationships with others. Partners having sexual relations will have a tendency to attach to each other's issues and carry them in their energy field five or six months, sometimes longer, even after a relationship has ended. It is best for partners involved in close relationships to work together in prayer and release work to help raise each other up and support each other's spiritual path.

Initially, partners have a tendency to look for self-interest in dating. The male looks for acceptance and appreciation. The female looks for support and financial success in a partner. Both partners are brought together through energies of physical attraction. In *A Course in Miracles,* Christ tells us that chemistry of partnership energies brings partners together, but for relationships to last, they have to evolve toward the purpose of the Holy Spirit. Pornography, fantasy, and sexual attraction are short-lived, and excitement has to evolve to caring and sharing for each other. Good loving and long-lasting relationships have partners being "into" each other. They leave behind superficial purposes and ulterior motivation of their own agendas. A healthier path of Higher Love through Spirit brings greater satisfaction and fulfillment.

When dark energies are about, the Bible says to proclaim, "Satan, get thee behind me!" There are also approaches calling in Archangel Michael for strength and empowerment of our personal truth, along with powerful

Archangel Khamael for clearing out unwanted energies and for balancing the energies of Archangel Michael. We also call in Archangel Tzadkiel for balancing energies of nurturing, fortification, and upbuilding forces of the Violet Flame of Transformation. We call Christ Holy Spirit for blessings, rejuvenation, illumination, and energies to transcend mass consciousness.

Archangel Haniel teaches us to overcome issues of emotions in order to live in grace. Archangel Raphael teaches us through initiation to carry consciousness of truth and healing. Archangel Gabriel brings purity to our energy fields and promotes communication between levels within. Gabriel also facilitates communication with higher levels of Spirit. Archangel Sandalphon helps to use Spirit in the physical.

In these treacherous times, there are health conditions inherent to aging, as well as diseases being unleashed in the world. What we don't know *can* hurt us or even shorten our life-span. It is mandatory for our health and well-being for each of us to do our own research on medical protocol, especially if the medical community has rushed to release unestablished solutions to biological threats. To help humanity, we may be recommending what we believe to be safe and effective solutions before enough studies have confirmed these solutions to be truly beneficial. This is in line with each person taking personal responsibility and following their own spiritual guidance.

Our main concern is bringing in Light to expand and empower our being, our expression, and our life-decisions. The Light consumes the darkness and forces it out of our energy field, bringing Higher Love to reach higher consciousness and bring grace into our lives. We are charged with holding a single focus of Love, Light, and compassion for ourselves and for humanity.

It is prudent to bring prayer and meditation through our heart, mind, body, and soul, making decisions based on the union of our mind, our intuition, and discernment with Spirit speaking to us from within our heart. We should always follow our highest guidance from Spirit, not from fear.

There are many energies in the world that are unfriendly to us, and it is important for each of us to maintain our higher vibration rate, our higher spiritual essence, that we continue making the healthiest right choices for ourselves. It is best to trust that the Light will prevail. We ask that Christ Holy Spirit and Angels break through the energies of illusion here on the physical plane, and give us clarity and strength. Our guidance will see us through all challenges and lead us in grace.

Dark energies may want to separate humanity from our soul-connection to God and our evolutionary path, but our heartfelt prayer, our faith, and our intimate meditation with Spirit keep us united and in strong union with soul and with God.

AS WE THINK, SO OUR LIFE GOES!

We create miracles with our prayers. We choose to manifest strength, vitality, empowerment, and success. Our strength is to know that Light will prevail over all things. Our willingness to accept expansion in awareness and growth of our spiritual essence, in sincerity, opens the doors to new potential and higher expression.

Our thinking also effects our health. "Stinking Thinking" causes our mental and emotional issues to be held in the body, causing health issues in the physical. By changing our thinking, we can choose release, clarity, and grace.

Even though we are aware that our energy field goes out into the world to attract people and experiences to us, we may lose track, from time to time, of just what powerful forces our intentions and our trust in God are—that they are actually creating our lives.

Often, our first reaction is to blame others for what we are experiencing. Our judgment of others makes us think we know who or what people are all about, or what situations are all about. If we use our spiritual discernment within our heart, we can decide if a person or situation is for us to release, and bless everyone in Light. Many times, just releasing an issue is all that is necessary to be at peace.

On our spiritual path, we maintain a meditative awareness with Spirit. Our faith and our trust in our oneness with God, goes beyond religion and a belief in prayer, and extends to a certainty that our prayers are answered. We come to know, beyond doubt, that we are empowered by our partnership with God.

We receive confirmation as we constantly remain open to hear guidance and stay open to receive miracles in our lives. The ways of Spirit are mysterious to us in the physical, but we see the signs all around us that our prayers are being answered. We know that God is always with us through all challenges.

We release our judgments, blame, and doubts stemming from the physical, and surrender our attachments to how and when our prayers are answered. We trust in the Light. We want to release our fears and *reactive* issues from the world around us. We become *proactive* as we honor our truth within and our empowerment with Spirit through Soul.

The Native American teaching views Light as the *gentle way,* known as the "Way of the Shaman." They refer to people using dark energies as coming from a place of "Power" that is manipulation coming from ego. The Native

American Indian sees the Great Spirit, Wakan-Tanka, much like we might see God the Father. They see Tunkhashila much like we might see Christ the Son. The many powers of Grandmother Earth, together, are like the Holy Spirit.

Dark forces are the harbingers of deception and sabotage. Best to align with Source God, the Mind of God, and combine with the ONE THING for miracles.

ALIGN THROUGH CHRIST LIGHT.

Always choose Christ Light as the truth of who we are! Align in a single focus of expression, and don't waiver or flip-flop. Faith in God is our strength within us. Ask Archangel Michael and Christ to close unwanted portals and invoke alignment with our highest Light. Say "NO" to unwanted energies!

WE LOOK TO THE LIGHT AND OUR TRUTH WITHIN
FOR GUIDANCE TO CARRY GRACE FORWARD
IN OUR LIFE AMIDST ADVERSITY
IN THE PHYSICAL WORLD.

In the Gnostic gospels, Hermes Trismegistus describes the attributes of the highest level of Light, the Mind of God. He describes the nature of Source God as the Essence of God—the Good, the Beautiful, the Wisdom, the Blessedness. These are the energies of Mind and Soul. Source-Mind has given inspiration, wisdom, and knowledge to Hermes Thrice-Great Trismegistus, and therefore to us through the teaching of all structure of creation.

The energies of Buddha are contained within all creation on Earth. We are reminded of this every time we see a picture of Buddha. The religion of Buddhism is about the energetic blessing of compassion relayed to us in the energies of Jorei through Avalokiteshavara and Chenrizig, and Reiki, being One with God.

The Hindu religion brings us purification through meditative discipline, and Christ Holy Spirit brings salvation through the sacrifice of Christ—the gift to humanity of forgiveness and acceptance. We pray for Christ Holy Spirit and the Grace of God.

We have already spoken about three different ranges of energy consciousness—all with different purposes—that we can use to serve us by raising our level of functioning, level of vibration, and level of understanding. Much more about these levels of consciousness are contained in *Prayers for All Occasions,* and *MYSTIC: Manifesting Your Soul, Truth in Consciousness.*

The first range is the set of energies contained in the chakra system. These energy centers, the purpose of each chakra vortex, and the energetic bodies connected to each, together make up the complex system of energies that stabilize our expression in the physical. Light is infused into each chakra from Spirit, supporting vitality and balancing our life-expression. Balance of Light into the physical through alignment with Light is our energetic support and empowerment. (Covered in more detail in *Prayers for All Occasions* in Chapter III: Chakras, Archangels, and Rays.)

The second range is contained in the Qabalah "TREE OF LIFE." Each sephira is an initiation representing stages of illumination of the soul. We descend into embodiment, integrating the spiritual insights acquired along the way. The archetypes and the symbolism in the TREE OF LIFE speak to us at a higher level of Spirit during meditation and dream time, orchestrated by the Light. (Covered in more detail in *Prayers for All Occasions* in Chapter VIII: Overview of the Sacred Energies and Light Beings.)

The third range of consciousness is associated with the grid system of the body and its relationship to Mother Earth. This includes the lay lines of Mother Earth, which are lines of energy connecting Sacred Sites of Spiritual Power. The grid lines have to do with energy flows that are connected with Mother Earth, and power spots that infuse Light from the etheric realms for the benefit and support of humankind. Some lines are in parallel and some are curved on the body. They can be activated using Axiatonal Therapy. (Covered in more detail in *MYSTIC: Manifesting Your Soul, Truth in Consciousness* in Chapter VII: Making a Shift in Our Lives)

A path of enlightenment involves frequent meditation, soul searching, being open to expansion in consciousness, and self-discovery.

We always align our lives vertically with the Light, Source God, which is Mind above, and then ground to Mother Earth below. In the name of Christ Holy Spirit, we call in the four cardinal directions on a horizontal plane. These are the archetypal, elemental energies of Earth forming a chalice to anchor higher Light in prayer. We bring in the Angels and Bringers of Light, with which we are intimately familiar, for blessings and prayer.

Sound and meditation lift us out of lower issues in the Earth plane, and take us to greater intimacy in prayer, transcending lower consciousness.

OUR ULTIMATE PURPOSE IN RELATIONSHIPS IS TO EXPERIENCE ISSUES THAT WE ALL SHARE FROM GROUP CONSCIOUSNESS, TO RELEASE FEELINGS IN UNCONDITIONAL LOVE, AND TO LIFT OURSELVES AND HUMANITY TO A HIGHER VIBRATION AND GRACE.

Prayer for Alignment Through Soul

We call our truth forward from within our heart
into perfect alignment with our Soul and Higher Self,
Divine Father and Mother God,
to the purest heart of all creation
and the All That Is!
We call ourselves into energetic connection with ground
for nurturing and support,
for balance between Spirit and the physical,
and for empowerment through alignment with Light!
We call in the four cardinal directions and Christ Holy Spirit plus
the Buddha consciousness and other religious affiliations.

We are always aware that there is a balance between masculine and feminine blessings of Spirit. Projection of inspiration is masculine creative force, and support is the feminine form of expression, how creation is expressed in all realms. There is also a balance between receiving in prayer and giving in service. There is balance in receiving flow of life vitality into our being, with infusion of higher Love, Light, creativity, and grace, blessing all humanity.

Manifesting Ceremony with Light

We turn problem areas, desires, and needs over to the Light for healing and change. We align with a powerful flow of Love and Light, consciously connecting with Father God above, the Truth within our Heart, and our loving Mother Earth below. This is our greatest Empowerment. Father God moves downward with insight and projection of our truth. Mother Earth moves upward as she totally nurtures and supports us. We each make a manifesting list to burn and release to the universe in prayer. We infuse these Sacred Energies into our being, uplifting our awareness.

The One

We call in the One God that is both Divine Mother and Divine Father—the "I Am That I Am," the "All That Is," the Good, the Beautiful, the Wisdom, the Blessedness from which all things have arisen by mediation or adaptation.

Light & Angels

*W*e center and ground in perfect alignment with Divine White Light, Christ Holy Spirit, and Mother Earth Empowerment.

Metatron is transformation. Archangel Michael is strength and protection. Melchizedek is profound healing. Lord Maitreya is beauty, bliss, and Lightness of being. We merge with them to know our Higher expression.

Creating Sacred Space, we honor the Four Sacred Directions, bringing Elements of Air from the East, Fire from the South, Water from the West, and Earth from the North. We call in Archangels Raphael, Michael, Gabriel and Uriel. We align with the Descending Light of Father Sky, Ascending Light of Mother Earth, and Spirit expressing the "Great Mystery" deep within our hearts. We are all Related!

We acknowledge their presence and give thanks from our heart!

Holy Flames

*W*e invoke the Ascension Flame, Saint Germain and the Violet Transmuting Flame, the Azure Blue Flame of Cause, the Pink Flame of Heart, the Emerald Green Flame of Healing.

Hebrew "Tree of Life" Ancient Wisdom

*W*e align with levels for creating: *Emanation, Creation, Formation,* and *Action.* As revealed to Hermes: the "One God" is everywhere and is our Highest Source. Highest Source contains the level of Aeon within it. Aeon contains the level of Cosmos within, including both *Time*, which is Change, and *Genesis*, which is Life and Death. The Energies of God are Mind and Soul. They are within all matter, and flow through our universe and planetary system with all the energies for life within. We give thanks for our blessings and consciously align on all levels. All energies flow from "One God" that is Divine Mother, Divine Father, and Holy Spirit, which is beyond our comprehension!

➢ PRAYER - *We* call Heaven and Earth into union of purpose. We unite with the greater purpose of our teachers, guides, Angels, and the Ascended Masters; all for our highest expression. We call forth the mighty forces of Love and Light for support, clarity and understanding. We join with Sacred 104 Lakota prayer energies. We give thanks from our hearts.

➢ VISUALIZATION - *We* see a brilliant vortex of Violet Light coming down from the heavens, through the center of our prayer circle, and anchoring into Mother Earth below, bringing Light into our Sacred Space and taking heaviness away.

➤ FORGIVING - *We* forgive ourselves for the illusion of imperfection. We release self-judgment. We send love and appreciation to everyone who has helped us to learn that *we are responsible for our own feelings.*

➤ GRATITUDE - *We* are in gratitude for Spirit working through our lives. We live with purpose and see our support and gifts coming to us as a natural extension of our lives. As we focus on the positive workings of Spirit, our lives expand even more. We put all challenges into the Light for resolution. We are blessed and accept support. We are prosperous. We are healthy, happy, whole, and balanced. We have inner peace and fulfillment in relationships with an open heart.

➤ BURNING CEREMONY - (Individually, we each say . . .) *We* dedicate ourselves to the highest expression of our being. We accept abundance and prosperity. We know everything that we need comes to us in perfect time, space, and sequence. We are making measurable changes in our lives through the flow of Light. We go forth with enthusiasm, excitement, and expectancy.

I AM THAT I AM!

One final prayer that is important to use is called a "shakti." This is a Hindu term that is a prayer that God or the Angels say *for us* that is permanently installed into our energy field. This prayer brings a blessing from a high source of Light, and may be a higher extension of our request to manifest our sole purpose that Hermes refers to as creating our Philosopher's Stone.

Light empowers every being on Earth. It's up to each individual to bring in acceptance of Light to dissolve victim and poverty consciousness, as well as toxic judgment from our low self-esteem and the way energies from others might be affecting us. If we believe an energy will take us down, then we have just given empowerment to that belief. Positive use of prayer and the medicine wheel technique expand the influence of Light in the world. Positive expression of our truth, blessing creation, and blessing humankind are all uplifting steps we can take to help raise mass consciousness and to make a difference.

Expansion of consciousness and higher adventure comes with walking our spiritual path. Our path is to transcend the challenges and pitfalls confronting us in the lower dimensions of the Earth plane.

Our lives become a continual living prayer emitting Light and raising the vibration of our spiritual essence. We are each actualizing our spiritual truth within our heart on our life's journey.

We are awakening to more peace, grace, joy, humor, vitality, rejuvenation, and fulfillment with miracles and synchronicities in our lives. We infuse Light into our worldly experiences.

We meditate for world peace and appreciation for Light coming to us, and we know that Spirit is always blessing us.

Vanities and dramas play out in lower dimensions, yet through our prayers and affirmations, the Light reorganizes the circumstances in and around our lives. We see that our higher purpose and miracles all manifest through us, and we have the time and resources to do everything we need and want in our lives.

We ask Spirit to show us how our lives are uplifted in Light. We see our prayers being answered every day! Thank you, God.

These techniques are all tools that we use with Spirit to assist in the lifting of our spiritual essence in our own process of evolution. We can pray directly to God, or through the Angels, for higher Light to help us with prayer and blessings to guide us.

INDIVIDUAL WITH GOD, ONE-ON-ONE IN ONE MIND
AND ONE THING, WITH THE FEW OR THE MANY,
I AM, WE ARE.

Preparing to receive directly from God, preparing to receive miracles, preparing to receive assimilation of blessings, wisdom, knowledge, and Love directly from God—this is your only job . . .

THE TEMPLE IS YOU!

Continue this amazing journey
with me in this
Bringing In the Light Series!

Visit my website at
www.AngelsGrace.org
to obtain more books in this series.

Prayers for All Occasions
BRINGING IN THE LIGHT SERIES
Book I

MYSTIC: Manifesting Your Soul, Truth In Consciousness
BRINGING IN THE LIGHT SERIES
Book II

The Temple Is YOU
BRINGING IN THE LIGHT SERIES
Book III

Make sure you have your copy of

For <u>all</u> occasions!

www.AngelsGrace.org

ABOUT THE AUTHOR

Author and Healer, John Pollock, is a "Bringer of Light" and energy worker, facilitating Cosmic Fire and Illumination to advance the quickening of spirit and personal transformation. His awakening and great heart connection enables him to hold a Sacred Space with Spirit for expansion and a shift in awareness!

The Temple is YOU is John's third book in his "Bringing in the Light" series, following *MYSTIC: Manifesting Your Soul, Truth In Consciousness* and the first of this series titled *Prayers for All Occasions.*

For more information about John's books and healing services, please visit his website at:

www.AngelsGrace.org

Made in the USA
Middletown, DE
24 June 2024

56228308R00152